T0328449

Cambridge Elements ≡

Elements in Religion and Monotheism
edited by
Paul K. Moser
Loyola University Chicago
Chad Meister
Bethel University

MONOTHEISM AND HUMAN NATURE

Andrew M. Bailey
Yale-NUS College

CAMBRIDGE
UNIVERSITY PRESS

CAMBRIDGE
UNIVERSITY PRESS

University Printing House, Cambridge CB2 8BS, United Kingdom

One Liberty Plaza, 20th Floor, New York, NY 10006, USA

477 Williamstown Road, Port Melbourne, VIC 3207, Australia

314–321, 3rd Floor, Plot 3, Splendor Forum, Jasola District Centre,
New Delhi – 110025, India

79 Anson Road, #06–04/06, Singapore 079906

Cambridge University Press is part of the University of Cambridge.

It furthers the University's mission by disseminating knowledge in the pursuit of
education, learning, and research at the highest international levels of excellence.

www.cambridge.org
Information on this title: www.cambridge.org/9781108964401
DOI: 10.1017/9781108966962

First published 2021

A catalogue record for this publication is available from the British Library.

ISBN 978-1-108-96440-1 Paperback
ISSN 2631-3014 (online)
ISSN 2631-3006 (print)

Monotheism and Human Nature

Elements in Religion and Monotheism

DOI: 10.1017/9781108966962
First published online: May 2021

Andrew M. Bailey
Yale-NUS College

Author for correspondence: Andrew M. Bailey, wrathius@gmail.com

Abstract: The main question of this Element is how the existence, supremacy, and uniqueness of an almighty and immaterial God bear on our own nature. It aims to uncover lessons about what we are by thinking about what God might be. A dominant theme is that Abrahamic monotheism is a surprisingly hospitable framework within which to defend and develop the view that we are wholly material beings. But the resulting materialism cannot be of any standard variety. It demands revisions and twists on the usual views. We can indeed learn about ourselves by learning about God. One thing we learn is that, though we are indeed wholly material beings, we're not nearly as ordinary as we might seem.

Keywords: monotheism, personal ontology, personal identity, materialism, dualism

ISBNs: 9781108964401 (PB), 9781108966962 (OC)
ISSNs: 2631-3014 (online), 2631-3006 (print)

Contents

1 Opening Moves

1.1 Abrahamic Philosophical Theology

This Element is about you and me. It is also about God.

You may find these topics incongruent. Though you and I are alike in various respects, what could we have in common with God? What does our nature have to do with that of the Almighty? Can a metaphysics of God illuminate a metaphysics of human nature? What can we learn about *us* by learning about the one true *God*?

These are the central questions of this Element. Before explaining their content, their significance, and the answers to come, some preliminary points are in order.

The topics at hand belong to philosophical theology. To do theology of any kind is to think about God. But one does not simply think about God. One uses various sources of evidence in building thoughts, comparing them, and evaluating them for coherence or plausibility. Would-be theologians face this question: *which* evidential sources are to be deployed? Some give a narrow answer and limit their attention to select texts as interpreted by a given tradition. Others take a more capacious approach and in addition to sacred texts freely consult deliverances of reason and the natural sciences. Structured approaches are possible too – one could take as evidence only what is revealed by reason while also taking certain dogmatic deliverances (from a midrash, creed, or hadith, say) as inviolable borders or absolute side-constraints. "Reason however you will about God," says this approach to philosophical theology, "provided that your conclusions respect orthodoxy so defined."

In this Element, I'll adopt a structured approach along these lines. But instead of submitting to sectarian dogma, I'll work within the Abrahamic tradition more broadly. I'll assume there is such a tradition – more on its content shortly – and that there are views about God on which Jews, Christians, and Muslims can all agree. The rule I'll attempt to follow may be expressed as this injunction: "Reason however you will about God, provided that your conclusions are consistent with the intersection of Islamic, Christian, and Jewish theology." For now, we can think of that intersection as centered around and including monotheism – the view that there is one God.[1]

Many – probably most – who endorse Abrahamic monotheism endorse quite a bit more besides; they endorse distinctively Jewish, Islamic, or Christian doctrines too. And any complete assessment of relevant evidence would have

---

[1] The term derives from More (1660), stylized there as "Monotheisme." For an illuminating treatment of its history since, see Herbener (2013).

to take those doctrines – and their own evidential status – into account. Perhaps doing all this would result in conclusions radically different from those I'll defend: a reasonable thought, and maybe even a worry. I invite readers with worries along these lines to take my arguments in this spirit: they reflect part of what "unaided reason" has to say on the matter. Perhaps a total assessment of the situation requires consulting revelation or tradition too. But the present study is one piece within that total assessment, and an important one in its own right. In accordance with the "unaided reason" dictum, my focus throughout will be abstract (on the ideas and how they hang together), rather than historical (who said what, and where, and when). My approach will, finally, be speculative. Rather than looking for definitive answers or airtight arguments, I'll attempt to find uncharted and fruitful conjectures that deserve further reflection and inquiry.

The questions at hand – questions about connections between *us* and *God* – deserve attention. Here's why. Beyond their intrinsic interest, they bear on a number of important issues across theology and philosophy. First, a growing cadre of avowed monotheists affirm views about human nature that significantly depart from majority views of their home traditions. In particular, many now lean toward *materialist* views about human nature according to which we are wholly material beings. The present study aids in determining whether it is internally coherent to conjoin such materialism with monotheism. Second, were monotheism to comport well with a particular theory of human nature, monotheists would thereby have reason to adopt that theory. Conversely, monotheism's supporting a particular view of human nature that is itself highly implausible would count against monotheism. Though this Element will not contend that monotheism is true, its arguments are still of interest to those who don't already accept monotheism; for its arguments may well bear on reasons to deny monotheism in the way noted previously. In inquiring about the *connections* between various doctrinal nodes, then, we can make progress in understanding which nodes are themselves worthy of assent.

The question of what we are, finally, bears on matters of grand and grave importance. We live and move and have our being in the vast world of nature. We are surrounded by material beings – plants and planets, rocks and trees, and much more besides. So, we are situated within nature in at least some important sense. But in what ways, exactly, are we continuous with nature and its other subjects? Are we full subjects in nature's kingdom, or just guests or permanent residents? I'd like to know the answers to these questions. And so, I wonder what we are. Inquiring into our connections with God is one way to make progress on that front.

You may at this point still be wondering how the being and oneness of God – monotheism, in a word – could speak to our own nature. Monotheism doesn't seem to say much about many *other* topics, after all. Learning that there is one God, does not, for example, seem to tell us much about the substance of mathematics or science – what properties are enjoyed by all primes over 737, say, or whether gold has a higher atomic number than titanium. There would thus seem to be secular truths – truths that monotheism gives us no reason to revise. Why should truths about our own nature be any different?

In a way, the entirety of this Element is an answer to that question. The arguments that follow will together illustrate in fairly specific ways how metaphysics of the divine bears on metaphysics of the human. But I can make two abstract observations even at the outset. First, monotheists tend to agree that we are made in the image of God, which certainly seems to imply that we are like God in important respects. And that would certainly seem to imply that one way to learn about ourselves is to learn about God – and vice versa. Second, a great many arguments about the metaphysics of human nature – about what we are and what we are like – deploy key premises about what sorts of things there are and what is possible. The existence and attributes of one Almighty God bear on those premises. For the view that there is one God should – and in fact does – make a difference to our sense of what exists and what is possible. And so monotheism turns out to bear on questions about us too.

1.2 Monotheism

The monotheism here in view comprises three core claims: the *existence*, *supremacy*, and *uniqueness* of God. Let's take them up in turn; each will receive more detailed treatment as appropriate in later sections.

God *exists*. There is an incorporeal spirit, distinct from the natural world and anything governed by its laws. God is not a material being. God is not a part of nature, nor is nature a part of God. The monotheism here in view, then, stands in sharp conflict with atheism, pantheism, and panentheism. If monotheism has two parts (the *mono* part and the *theism* part) this is the theism part.

God is *supreme*. Though God is distinct from the natural world, God created it all and enjoys unsurpassed power over all of concrete reality. This doctrine of supremacy gives some content to the *mono* part of *monotheism*. For it specifies a sense in which God is singular. God is not just a god (whether alone or among many). Nor is God yet another (albeit unusually potent) being subject to the laws of nature. The monotheism here in view, then, contrasts with both polytheism and what we might call *demiurge theism*, the doctrine that swaths of the natural world were uncreated and that a god somehow worked with them to shape the world as we know it.

God is, finally, *unique*. In particular, God is *one*. Astute readers will notice that this slogan may be ambiguous between a thesis about God's simplicity – God has no parts – and God's number – there is one God. I will, in due time, describe more detailed specifications of the uniqueness of God and address that apparent ambiguity. For now, we can think of uniqueness as the thesis that God is not many, whether in number or in any other sense. The doctrine of uniqueness gives further content to the *mono* part of *monotheism*. It, too, contrasts with polytheism.

These three elements together also contrast with what we might call *mere animism*, according to which the world is inhabited by various spirits that each enjoy a natural domain of proper authority and limited control (one in command of a waterfall, another in command of a forest, say). For the God here in view is not tied to particular regions of space and time, nor is God's power or proper authority limited. God's domain is complete.

God exists, God is supreme, and God is unique. Thus monotheism in bare outline. We turn now to rather less exalted subject matter: ourselves.

1.3 Human Nature

What are we? The question, despite its concision, *sounds* deep. But what is it asking and how might it be answered?

One could – perhaps under the influence of various "no self" doctrines – respond by denying that we are anything at all. I shall in what follows presuppose that this approach is mistaken. I shall presuppose that we exist. You are something. So am I. More generally, there are such things as people. This presupposition seems to be a safe bet. It is not, for one, a controversial thesis in at least this important sense: those who disagree with me here maintain that no one disagrees with me. They instead think that no one disagrees with anyone, since there's no one there to do the disagreeing. If uncontroversial theses in this sense are fair to presuppose, then mine is fair as any.

The presupposition at hand is limited. In supposing that we exist, I am not thereby supposing that we have or are in any sense unchanging selves, that we enjoy stable and informative criteria of identity over time, that we enjoy a mind-independent mode of existence, that we are fundamental items within the world, or that we are or have souls.

The presupposition that we exist is also defensible; it need not be a mere presupposition, though I'm content to treat it that way if necessary. Here is a brief demonstration. Premise: you are a human person. Conclusion: therefore, something is a human person. The premise seems true. You can think and feel; you have preferred personal pronouns; you can be appropriately addressed with "you" (proof of the premise: I just did so). So you are a person. And you are a human person (you're not, I presume, a Vulcan, an angel, or even an unusually sensitive brown bear). The conclusion follows from the premise. And the conclusion is equivalent to what I mean when I say that human persons exist. I conclude that the general presupposition at hand – that we exist – is innocuous, defensible, and true.

We exist. We are. But the question remains: *what* are we? And what are we asking when we ask *that* question? It will be helpful to separate three interconnected sub-questions:

– What is our ontological category? (category)
– Do we belong to that category as a matter of necessity? (modality)
– How do our mental properties relate to the physical properties of our bodies? (mentality)

I will now explain these sub-questions in more detail.

Category

We are concerned with the metaphysics of human nature. Our present inquiry thus differs in kind from other possible answers or approaches to the question of what we are – from the approaches of ethics, history, biology, or speculative futurology for example. We seek a special kind of truth about human persons; not just any will do. The claims that *we are each no more than 4,300 years old, we each have at least one great-grandparent, we are morally pluripotent beings capable of great good and of great evil* or that *we are beings that make tools and love and war* do not answer the question of what we are. They report truths about us, to be sure, but not truths of the right kind. For the question we're after, I propose, can only be answered by placing us within an ontological category.

To speak of ontological categories is to do metaphysics in the grand old style. It is to specify at the highest level of abstraction how reality divides. Consider, for example, a theory of ontological categories expressed in Figure 1.[2]

Charts don't always report doctrines. But this one does. According to the theory charted in Figure 1, for example, every item at all is a thing. There is no non-thing category, and no category higher than "thing." Similarly, every thing is either a property or an object, and every object is either material or immaterial. Both material and immaterial objects, furthermore, cleave into thinking and unthinking categories. We could also offer purported examples of items within

---

[2] On categories and their role in ontology, see van Inwagen (2014).

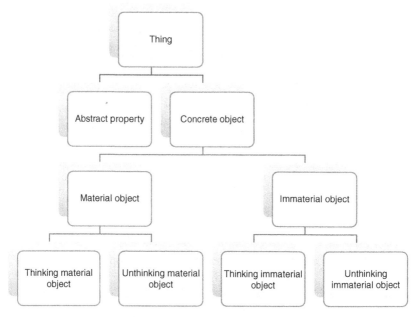

Figure 1 A categorical ontology

each of the four base-level categories (conscious organisms as thinking material objects; rocks as unthinking material objects; angels and demons as thinking immaterial objects; holes as unthinking immaterial objects).

The theory of ontological categories charted here does not settle questions about our nature. It does not say what we are. But it does furnish us with a useful tool for so doing. If you wanted to say what we were, using the chart, it's plain how you'd proceed: point to a node, and say "that's our place in this world; we're *those* things."

Two views about the category we belong to are of special interest and will command special attention in this study. The first – materialism about human persons (henceforth just "materialism") – says that we are thinking material objects. The second – dualism – denies this and says that we are thinking objects that are either partly or wholly immaterial.

Modality

I have distinguished truths about us that do not address the question of what we are from those that do. Here is one way of making this distinction more precise. Perhaps the former are merely contingent truths, while the latter are necessary. It is *true* that we are all to be found somewhere near the surface of planet Earth. But that truth is contingent – we could have been found elsewhere – and so does not, despite its grammatical form, say what we are. The hypothesis that each of us is necessarily a rational animal, goes the thought, is much closer to saying what we are because it tries to say more than what we happen to be – it tries to say what we *must be*.

This thought – that necessary truths are a vital element in answering the question of what we are – is not without some initial plausibility. It's unsurprising, then, that many have thought that if we fall under a given ontological category, we do so of necessity. So if we are immaterial thinking things, for example, then we *must* be immaterial thinking things. But modal claims along these lines are, as we'll see, not the only game in town. For now, though, I observe this: necessity and contingency here mark one dimension to the question of what we are. Whichever way one goes along that dimension, to speak to this matter is to specify more closely what we are by saying, if we are a given kind of item, whether we *had* to be that kind of item.

Mentality

You are a human person. You can think. You can feel. You can move about in the world and do all sorts of other interesting things. And you accomplish a great many of these feats with or through your body. You would, at least, be hard pressed to get by without it.

So let's talk next about your body. Your body exists in space and time. It is among your closest associates. You see it when you look in the mirror. Go ahead; take a look. Where it goes, you go. And, one thinks, where you go, it must follow. Indeed, you can make it move through sheer force of will. You bear, in sum, an important and intimate relation to a certain material object.

You are not alone in having a body. I have one too; lucky me. In fact, we all do, it seems. And we each bear some intimate relation to these bodies of ours.

This relation invites – and has received – explication. Some say that we are brains, and thus relate to our bodies by being *parts* of them. Others say that we *are* our bodies. Some say we have, in addition to our bodies, a certain immaterial part – a *soul*. And yet others say that we just *are* immaterial souls and bear some special relation short of identity to our bodies – perhaps we inhabit and control them despite not being them. Each of these views answers a specification of the question of what we are. They answer that question by specifying *how* we relate to our bodies. They thus address a dimension of the question of what we are.

The question of how we relate to our bodies – by inhabitation, identity, parthood, or in some other way – has broader import. For saying, how we relate to our bodies says how we fit into reality and its categories in the broadest possible sense. To say how we relate to our bodies is to begin answering the category question. That is the point explained previously. But there's another question here as well.

Your body enjoys a host of biological, chemical, and physical features. And its parts – electrons, cells, organs, flesh and bone – are mutually entangled in a web of biological, chemical, and physical relations. Understanding their workings is the business of chemistry, biology, physics, neurology, and so on.

You also have a mental life. You believe, perceive, and feel. There is something it is like to be you. You have a perspective on things. Understanding the workings of your mind is the business of classical psychology and related disciplines.

Thus there are some domains into which you fall – physical and mental. How do these domains relate, though? Are they two, one, or something else? We can put the question a little differently. There must be, many have thought, *some* systematic relation between these biological, chemical, and physical properties – of your body or its parts – and your own mental life. Your own thoughts and perceptions and feelings crucially involve these somatic properties. But how?

There is some intimate relation here between the mental and the physical. And it too invites – and has received – explication. Some say that our mental properties *are* physical properties of our bodies. So when you believe that the sum of two and two is four, for example, that belief just is a state of your body (or your brain, or some other material item). Some say that the somatic properties somehow *constitute* or *ground* the mental properties. And some say that physical properties of our bodies or their parts *cause, but are distinct from* our mental properties. And there are other views besides. The point is this: saying how our mental properties relate to the physical properties of our bodies and their parts is a third and final dimension to the question of what we are. To say how our mental life fits into nature – and reality more broadly – is one more way of saying what we are.

I've identified three dimensions or specifications of the question of what we are. A satisfactory answer to the broader question will address all of them. It will situate us within some ontological category or other; it will say whether we belong there of necessity; and it will say how our mental properties relate to the physical properties of our bodies or their parts. These are distinct but mutually supporting tasks.

1.4 Preview

There aren't just *views* about what we are. There are also a bevy of *arguments*. These arguments purport to show what category we fall under, whether we do so of necessity, and what relation binds our mental lives to the activity of the material world.

We are now in a position to more sharply state the questions central to this Element: how does the existence, supremacy, and uniqueness of God bear on these arguments? Suppose there is one God, supreme and unique: what can we then learn about the arguments that purport to show that we are, for example, wholly material or wholly immaterial beings? That our mental lives wholly derive from – or are perhaps entirely untethered to – the activity of the material world?

Those are the questions. Now some answers and a preview of the arguments to come. In Sections 2 and 3, I'll evaluate the prospects for views according to which we are luminous spiritual beings. Though monotheism is indeed a hospitable environment for such views, I'll argue that it also offers resources to undercut some of the usual arguments (and one unusual but intriguing argument that begins with the very concept of a spirit). In Section 4, I will more carefully develop the uniqueness element of monotheism and show that it uncovers a dilemma for anyone who'd argue for any conclusion at all from theological premises. In short: if God is truly and absolutely one in the most demanding sense, then we cannot be like God in any sense. I close the study, in Section 5, by considering and rejecting a *normative* conception of God's uniqueness according to which God alone is infinitely valuable. Having done that, I evaluate the prospects for views according to which we are wholly material beings. I'll argue that the usual suite of arguments along these lines fail, given monotheism. This is perhaps unsurprising. What's more surprising is that heterodox forms of materialism can survive within and indeed cohere well with monotheism. The evidence favors, I'll argue, a *magical*, *plastic*, and *singular* view according to which, though our mental lives do not robustly depend on the workings of the material world, though our nature is highly contingent, and though we figure into the laws of nature in a unique way, we are nonetheless wholly material beings. We are indeed subjects within nature's kingdom. But we're special too.

2 Spirits Human and Divine

2.1 Beyond Nature

If the cosmos is all there is, or was, or ever will be, then there is no God. Nor is there anything like God. All things are, instead, full subjects of nature – bound by nature's laws, born within and confined to space and time, destined to remain there for all their days. And all facts about concrete reality are rooted in facts about these natural denizens; no danglers lurk outside the realm. This is one way to think about the world and its contents – in a word, *naturalism.*

But if there is, as monotheists suppose, one true God – a supreme incorporeal being who brought that cosmos into existence, then new possibilities emerge. God is a wedge that cracks open our sense of what kinds of things there could be and what reality must be like. For when naturalism is set aside, we need not take the cosmos and its visible furniture – stars, trees, steel beams, and so on – as exhausting reality, or even as paradigms of it. Perhaps there is something more. And perhaps that something more is an item in addition to the Almighty; perhaps there are other beings *like* God in various respects. The assumption of monotheism and the rejection of naturalism invite speculation in this direction.

And so we descend once again to the less exalted subject of ourselves. Might we be, like God, rather different from the other furniture of the cosmos? Might we be spirits too?

Here is an inchoate suspicion: if the Almighty is an incorporeal spirit, then so are we. Or, at least, monotheism is an unusually hospitable framework for the view that we, too, are luminous spiritual beings. In the discussion to come, I'll consider two answers that take us beyond mere suspicion and into the realm of argument. The first begins with the idea that, on monotheism, spirits – incorporeal thinking beings – are *possible*, and supposes that we could have been among them. From this possibility, the argument extracts the conclusion that we are in fact incorporeal thinking beings. The second argument doesn't require that we could have been spirits, or even that they are possible. It instead begins with the simple but controversial assumption that we have the concept of a spirit. And it concludes from that conceptual assumption that we are in fact spirits.

Both arguments begin with premises that the monotheist endorses and move to conclusions about what we are. After developing some terminology and making a few assumptions explicit, I'll contend that they both fail.

2.2 Matter and Spirit

All of this business about spirits and such may rightly prompt suspicion. And though I do not have rigorous definitions of the key ideas here – mentality, material object, human person, spirit – a few remarks will help us focus attention on a common object.

I'll say that someone thinks if and only if they either believe, fear, doubt, desire, or hope – or are conscious: in a state where there is something it is like to be in that state. You are thinking when you hope for rain or when you feel pain, for example. And I'll say something is wholly material if and only if it is at some level or other composed of items, all of which have narrowly physical properties (properties that figure into fundamental physics) and none of which think. The idea here is roughly that to be entirely material is to have parts at some level or other that are characterized by fundamental physics, but that do not themselves exhibit any mentality (this second condition rules out various kinds of idealism). Rocks, sheets of paper, and arm bracers, one suspects, satisfy this condition, for all are composed of parts treated by fundamental physics that do not think. Spirits, angels, demons, and gods are rather different; for at every level they have parts (or are themselves things) that either think or are not characterized by fundamental physics.

Human persons are those things to which we ordinarily refer with first-person pronouns.[3] Among human persons are those things we sometimes call "logicians," "boomers," "heterosexuals," and "student-athletes." You are a human person. So am I.

Materialism about human persons (henceforth, materialism) is the thesis that we human persons are wholly material; pure dualism (henceforth, dualism) is the competing claim that we are wholly immaterial. Note that we are here concerned mostly with materialism in this narrow sense – materialism about *us* (as opposed to a wider thesis according to which all concrete things are wholly material – a thesis that seems plainly incompatible with the existence of an incorporeal God and which would be an expression of the competing naturalist stance with which this Section began).

As we'll think of things in the sequel, a spirit is just a wholly immaterial thing – or, as I'll sometimes say, an incorporeal thing – that thinks. Dualism, then, may also be stated as the view that we are spirits. To say that something is a spirit, note, is not to say that it is a ghost, an item somehow made of spiritual stuff – ectoplasmic goo or whatnot – or to be found within space or time. A spirit is simply a wholly immaterial being that thinks.

2.3 Divine Thinking

Many monotheists say that God thinks. This is what they express, I think, when they say that God believes various things (all truths, for example) or that God is angry at wickedness, or that God desires that none should perish, or that God is sad when people do bad things. I suspect this divine mentality also follows from other features attributed to God. A god that neither hopes nor desires nor believes could not keep promises or be jealous, forgiving, joyful, patient, holy, just, wise, or good.

In a word, God is a spirit.

---

[3] van Inwagen (2002).

The assumption at hand – that God thinks – is, as we'll see later, eminently deniable. Indeed, it has been denied. But in the present Section and the one to follow, we'll pursue this question: suppose there is one God who thinks. Suppose God is, in our sense, a spirit. What follows for the metaphysics of human nature? What truths can this doctrine uncover about *us*?

That was all a bit abstract. Here is a striking quotation that will help us think of things more concretely:

> God leads a very interesting life ... he is full of joy. Undoubtedly he is the most joyous being in the universe ... While I was teaching in South Africa some time ago, a young man ... took me out to see the beaches near his home in Port Elizabeth. I was totally unprepared for the experience. I had seen beaches, or so I thought. But when we came over the rise where the sea and land opened up to us, I stood in stunned silence and then slowly walked toward the waves. Words cannot capture the view that confronted me. I saw space and light and texture and color and power ... that seemed hardly of this earth. Gradually there crept into my mind the realization that God sees this all the time. He sees it, experiences it, knows it from every possible point of view, this and billions of other scenes like and unlike it, in this and billions of other worlds. Great tidal waves of joy must constantly wash through his being. It is perhaps strange to say, but suddenly I was extremely happy for God and thought I had some sense of what an infinitely joyous consciousness he is and of what it might have meant for him to look at his creation and find it "very good." We pay a lot of money to get a tank with a few tropical fish in it and never tire of looking at their brilliant iridescence and marvelous forms and movements. But God has seas full of them, which he constantly enjoys. (I can hardly take in these beautiful little creatures one at a time.) ... This is what we must think of when we hear theologians and philosophers speak of him as a perfect being. This is his life.[4]

This is a remarkable and confounding passage. First, it suggests that God has a mental life full of color, texture, and sound. God doesn't just know that the sum of two and two is four; God experiences – with joy unbounded – the sea and the sun and the rest of the cosmos too. One could affirm divine mentality without going this far, of course – perhaps God believes truths and intends good outcomes without enjoying any temporal (much less sensory or emotional) experience at all.[5] The view here is extreme. But it does give vivid expression to one specification of divine mentality. Second, the passage also points toward both affinity and distance between the mental lives we enjoy and God's own. We know what it's like to view some tropical fish in a tank. God sees all the fish at once, we're told. So God's experience is somehow like ours, but

---

[4] Willard (1999, pp. 62–63).

[5] For rigorous treatment and exploration of divine emotion in particular, see Mullins (2020).

also a radical extension or expansion of it. What is it like to see all the fish all at once, and from every possible angle? Is that like watching a billion television monitors at once? Or seeing the world through an unusually wide-angle lens? Or something else? Answers here are less than forthcoming – and the questions themselves are a bit mysterious. Perhaps rightly so: philosophy of mind is hard; philosophy of the divine mind, harder still.

Some will react to these suggestions with disdain or even horror. They will see the portrayal of God here as anthropomorphic at best – and idolatrous at worst. Others will react with wonder or awe. Either way, we are in the right mood for inquiry into possible connections between minds human and divine.

2.4 Incorporeal People

Consider your average material object – a rock, say. Could it exist without being entirely made of matter? Many have thought not. Rocks are not only wholly material beings; they have to be wholly material. That thought can be extended; and, applied to us, it says that if we are wholly material beings, we had to be such. On this theory, our nature is in a certain sense *rigid* or inflexible.

It takes just one more ingredient to move from this rigid answer to the modality question – a conviction that if we fall within a certain ontological category we *must* fall within it – to a dualist answer to the category question – to the view that we are spirits. The extra ingredient is this: we could have been immaterial; each of us is possibly even if not in fact, a spirit.

The ingredients combine to form a classic argument for dualism. It goes like this:

> (i) I could exist without being wholly material. (ii) But if something is wholly material, it must be wholly material. So I am not identical to anything that is, in fact, wholly material. So I am not identical to my living body, to my brain, or to any other such item.[6]

Monotheism provides some motivation for the first premise, for monotheists think that spirits are possible in the first place. And with that possibility in hand, it is not hard to conclude that we could have been spirits ourselves: just imagine yourself existing, goes the thought, but without any body at all.

It's a potent and intriguing argument. Materialists have typically attempted to resist its first premise. I'm now going to show, however, that there is another

---

[6] Historical antecedents of this argument include Descartes's sixth meditation and Avicenna's Floating Man thought experiment. Contemporary formulations include Hart (1988, p. 141), Lowe (2000, pp. 10–11), Plantinga (1974, pp. 67–68), Plantinga (2006), Plantinga (2007), Swinburne (1997, p. 154), Taliaferro (1994, p. 205), and Taliaferro (1997).

way. Monotheism, in fact, provides resources with which to resist the second premise.

I begin with a thought experiment. It will be somewhat speculative; I don't expect what I say here to command universal assent. But the exercise will still illustrate, I hope, that adding God to the picture changes our sense of what is possible and thus our evaluation of arguments for dualism.

Bradley is a living organism. Bradley has, at some very low level, a host of tiny physical items as his only parts – atoms, we'll call them. The atoms are, through a complex network of causal dispositions, integrated and united in various ways and so compose Bradley himself. One day, God annihilates one of Bradley's atoms and replaces it with an angelic surrogate. "In situations where the atom would have pushed," God tells Gabriel, "push. So also for pulling and electromagnetic interaction and distorting the geometry of space-time and so on." Gabriel does as he's told. To the unsuspecting outsider, Bradley looks and smells and behaves exactly as he did before. But Bradley has a new part: Gabriel plays those causal roles once occupied by the atom he supplanted, and so exhibits the integration and unity required to count as a part of Bradley.

It happens again, and again, and again. There are plenty of angels to go around. And in the fullness of time – many months, say – the transformation is complete. Bradley is, at some very low level, composed entirely of angels (at higher levels he remains composed, of course, of cells; and at yet higher levels perhaps of organs). Every atom has been replaced, and its role exactly mimicked by a new angelic surrogate. Angels are wholly immaterial items. Bradley is, at some very low level, composed entirely of wholly immaterial items. So Bradley is, in his final form, wholly immaterial.

If the thought experiment here is possible, then it is possible for a wholly material being to become wholly immaterial. The scenario makes some substantive assumptions, including:

1. It is possible for spirits to interact with the natural world. God – or an angel, at God's command – can, for example, push and pull or distort the geometry of spacetime.
2. Causal integration makes for parthood. If something assumes an atom's role in a complex network of causal relations, it becomes part of the greater whole just as the atom was.
3. If something is, at some very low level, composed entirely of wholly immaterial thinking beings, then it is itself wholly immaterial.
4. Something can survive the replacement of one part with a surrogate that exactly duplicates that part's causal role.

I do not claim that these assumptions are ironclad. But they have some initial plausibility and special dialectical traction within a monotheistic framework. The first assumption is the most contentious. It is also a consequence of monotheism – if there is an incorporeal almighty God who brought the cosmos into being, then it is possible for immaterial items to interact with the material world.[7] The second is a consequence of many leading theories of parthood and composition.[8] The third is a straightforward consequence of plausible accounts of what it is to be wholly material in the first place.[9] Something composed of thinking spiritual beings simply doesn't count as wholly material. The fourth is, finally, an extension of the second assumption along with the plausible auxiliary hypothesis that it is at least possible for some things to gain or lose parts; your body testifies to this auxiliary hypothesis every time it survives a meal or a haircut.

We can put the point a bit more abstractly: if God is supreme and can interact with and command the material world at will, then a great many more things will seem possible than one might otherwise guess. When monotheism is assumed – and here theism alone won't do the trick; one really needs God *supreme* – then thought experiments like the one I've proposed will seem much more plausible. Monotheism makes a difference to what's possible and thus to metaphysics.

The materialist typically denies the first premise of the argument. But this is not mandatory. One may, instead, claim that the second premise is false; that something is in fact wholly material doesn't imply that it must be wholly material. For, as the thought experiment reveals, it is possible for a wholly material being to transform into a wholly immaterial being. This response is dialectically strong in two ways. First, it exploits one of the dualist's most distinctive commitments: the assumption that material and immaterial things can interact. So the dualist is hardly in a position to resist that stage of the argument. The dualist who endorses monotheism faces even stronger pressure here to endorse that assumption. For without it, it is hard to maintain the supremacy of God as witnessed by the creation of the cosmos. Second, instead of merely calling into question or undercutting the second premise, it supplies a positive reason to reject that premise.[10]

One might speculate that, despite coming to be made of angels, Bradley in his final form still has a body. If the angels are doing their job, after all, Bradley can still be seen or injured or smelt, for example. And Bradley remains composed, at

---

[7] See Kim (2005, pp. 70–92) and replies in Audi (2011) and Owen (forthcoming). On conservation laws and interaction, see Cucu & Pitts (2019).

[8] van Inwagen (1990), Bowers (2019), and Hoffman & Rosenkrantz (1997).

[9] Bailey (2020b) and Ney (2008).   [10] Merricks (1994) and Cole & Foelber (1984).

one level, of cells; at another, of organs. This may well be correct. But note: Bradley's "body" is radically unlike any other. Paradigm material objects – rocks, for example – are, at some very low level, composed strictly of unthinking items that obey laws of physics. Electrons and such. Not so for Bradley. At that very low level, Bradley is composed of beings that, in contrast to electrons and such, think – angelic spirits – and that needn't obey laws of physics in the way that electrons do. My own reaction here is to affirm, on those grounds, that Bradley in his final form is no longer wholly material and is in fact wholly immaterial. That Bradley remains composed of cells or of organs, finally, doesn't show that he's still a material being after the transformation. It shows that Bradley's cells or organs – like their host organisms – can themselves become wholly immaterial.

Bradley exists at the beginning of the thought experiment. Does he cease to exist somewhere along the way? I doubt it. For the transformation takes place over many months. And each new surrogate angel exactly mimics the atom it replaces; it takes on all of the causal roles played by that atom and so finds integration into the broader network of atoms. If organisms can survive taking in new parts by, say, eating them – and it seems they can, precisely when and because new atoms become causally integrated with old atoms – then Bradley can survive his angelic transformation too.

Here is another consequence of my thesis. A great many dualists assume that their view is necessarily true if true at all. They assume that if we are in fact wholly immaterial then we must be wholly immaterial. In light of the argument I've given, this answer to the modality question is not convincing. Indeed, it is false. I've given a thought experiment in which Bradley, a living human organism, transforms from matter into spirit. And nothing I've said crucially relies on Bradley's being an organism. He might just as well have been a brain, or a cerebral hemisphere, or whatever else it is that materialists about human persons say we are. The point is this: even if we are in fact wholly immaterial, we didn't have to be that way.

2.5 From Concept to Reality

The argument discussed here proceeded from the possibility of spirits to their reality and indeed to the conviction that we are among them. That argument was something of a classic. I'll now consider a less widely discussed (but no less fascinating) line of reasoning. This one begins with an even weaker assumption: that we have the concept of a spirit. It extracts from this simple claim the conclusion that the concept has purchase with respect to *us*, that we are in fact spirits. This argument, too, begins with a premise toward which monotheists will be friendly and that some naturalists reject.[11] For in affirming the existence of a spirit – God – monotheists would seem to be deploying the concept of one.[12]

Here's the argument in a nutshell: we can grasp, in broad outline at least, what it is to be a thinking immaterial thing or spirit. So it would seem that we can distinguish the concept of a spirit from that of a thinking material object. But there is, in fact, no way to coherently make that distinction. So there are not, after all, any thinking material objects, and we are ourselves spirits instead. That's the quick version of what I'll call the spirit concept argument. Here's a more careful presentation from J. P. Moreland:

> (i) If someone understands what it is for something to be an entity (or purported entity) – a divine spirit, for example – then she has a distinct, positive concept of that thing. (ii) We understand what it is for God to be a divine spirit. Therefore, we have a distinct, positive concept of God's being a divine spirit. (iii) If thinking matter is possible, it is not the case that we have a distinct, positive concept of God's being a divine spirit. Therefore, it is not the case that thinking matter is possible. (iv) We are either thinking material beings or spirits. Therefore, we are spirits.[13]

The third premise is clearly in need of further explanation; I'll say more about it presently, but first some more-general comments.

The spirit concept argument is all about concepts. You may be leery, and rightly so. But in this case, a permissive attitude is in order, for the argument can be translated into other vocabulary. Instead of talking about "having a concept," for example, we might instead talk about "competently using words like 'spirit,'" "understanding what it is to be a spirit," "knowing what property the word 'spirit' expresses," and the like. So even though the argument at hand is unashamedly conceptual, it needn't assume that guise.

The spirit concept argument can, at first glance, seem to be a bit of a magic trick. It appears to pull a thick thesis about what we are from a remarkably thin conceptual hat. I think it is more than just a trick, though, in at least this sense: reflection on the argument is instructive. Just as tricky ontological arguments invite research on the nature of modality, so too the spirit concept argument invites excursion into the jungle of ontological categories and their relation to our basic concepts. Even if the argument turns out to be unsound, it will still have been worth our time.

Since the spirit concept argument isn't one of those classic arguments one reads in textbooks, let me briefly say why I'm giving it attention here. The

---

[11] Smith & Jones (1986, pp. 46–49)   [12] This section adapts material from Bailey (2017).

[13] The wording here is mostly from Moreland (2013, p. 36), with a few simplifying and stylistic amendments.

argument caters to a wide audience. It targets anyone who thinks they have a concept of a spirit. Those who think God exists or who do positive theology about God (all of whom would have a concept of a spirit, I suppose) have reason to pay attention. The argument is ambitious in its conclusion, claiming nothing less than that we are wholly immaterial thinking things, giving us further reason to pay attention. It is surprisingly modest in its premises, beginning from seemingly innocuous ideas about concepts and their place in our intellectual economy. Each premise seems plausible and appealing. And yet together the premises imply a surprising metaphysical result – a sure sign that a closer look is in order. The spirit concept argument is of special interest for the present study, finally, since one of our goals is to examine the coherence of joining materialism about *us* with conviction that there is a mighty immaterial spirit – God.

The first premise includes a strict requirement: a concept is adequate only if it is positive. Let's call this the Positive Requirement. Moreland's case for the Positive Requirement opens: "if one has an adequate concept of, say, a type of entity (e.g. being an animal, being a mammal, being a dog), this entails that one has a positive concept of the features unique to the entities that fall within the extension of that concept."[14]

Moreland does not offer an account of what it is for a concept to be positive. Nor does he elaborate on what adequacy might here amount to ("adequate for what purpose?" one wonders). Some might raise a fuss and turn these nagging worries into objections. I'm willing to set these details aside, though, since I think the premise is false in broad outline (and not just in detail).

Here's why. We have an adequate concept of the abstract. We possess the concept of abstractness. We use it in theorizing and appear to do so with full competence. We can reliably classify items as either abstract or concrete. People and planets are concrete, while numbers and propositions are abstract. And yet there is very little we can say to explain what abstractness comes to.[15] We can say only what it is not. So, for example, if concreteness is a matter of having causal powers, abstractness is a matter of lacking them. Similarly, if concreteness is a matter of being in space and time, abstractness is a matter of not being within space and time. When it comes to understanding the abstract and concrete, other roads are closed, and so we travel the *via negativa*. There is, then, a convincing counterexample to the Positive Requirement; we have an adequate concept of the abstract, but it is not a positive concept.

Moreland correctly anticipates the objection; he suggests "real/unreal, true/false, good/evil, male/female" as potential problem cases. In reply, he distinguishes two varieties of concept pairs. In the first variety (priority pairs, let us

---

[14] Moreland (2013, p. 37).   [15] Rosen (2012).

say), one concept is more "conceptually basic and the other is a privation of some sort or another (real/unreal, true/false, good/evil)."[16] In the second variety (egalitarian pairs, let us say), neither concept is more basic, nor is either a privation of the other. One interesting (and perhaps distinguishing) feature of egalitarian pairs is this: each member of the pair has its own positive concept.

Moreland then argues that spirit/matter is not a priority pair. It is not as though the concept of a spirit is merely the concept of non-matter, for "the number two satisfies this privation condition [non-matter] but it is not a spirit."[17] So spirit/matter must, instead, be an egalitarian pair, and, accordingly, "there needs to be a distinct positive concept of matter and spirit for there to be an adequate concept of each."[18]

In reply, I note that the conclusion Moreland appears to draw here (that spirit/matter is an egalitarian pair) does not follow from the premise (that the concept of a spirit is not merely the concept of non-matter). Here is what does follow: spirit and matter do not exhaustively and exclusively chop up reality. For it is possible for something to be non-matter without being a spirit (this is what the example of the number two illustrates). Moreland's reasoning here fails to establish that spirit/matter is an egalitarian pair; it thus does not support the thesis that "there needs to be a distinct positive concept of matter and spirit for there to be an adequate concept of each."

It's now time to connect all this to the theory of categories discussed in Section 1.3. To give a theory of categories is do ontology in the grandest and most ambitious sense, recall. It is to say, in the broadest possible terms, what the joints of reality come to. Consider the ontology disclosed in Figure 1 (Section 1.3). The Chart Ontology is coherent. It may not be true. But it is coherent. And to talk about the Chart Ontology is obviously to do ontology (a point that will prove important in the following). To argue about whether the Chart Ontology is true is to argue about what, in the broadest possible terms, the joints of reality come to.

Reflection on the Chart Ontology can illuminate the Positive Requirement's failure. Here's how. Every juncture within the Chart Ontology involves a concept and its complement. The highest juncture involves the concept concrete and its complement, abstract. The second-highest junctures involve the concept material and its complement, immaterial. And the third-highest junctures involve the concept of thinking and not-thinking. These are all perfectly serviceable concepts, so far as I can tell; they are adequate. The Chart Ontology is, after all, coherent. But half of them appear to be negative. So there cannot be any general requirement that adequate concepts be positive.

---

[16] Moreland (2013, p. 37).   [17] Moreland (2013, p. 38).   [18] Moreland (2013, p. 38).

Consider this reply: There is, I'll concede, some loose and disreputable sense in which we have and may freely or usefully deploy negative concepts. You may talk about non-dogs all you like, for example, and in doing so may even say some true and useful things. But for the serious business of carving up reality and specifying what things are, we're best served by using only positive concepts.

The reply is tempting. But not for students of the Chart Ontology – or anyone who recognizes what the Chart ontologists are up so. For students of the Chart Ontology are engaged in the serious business of carving up reality. They are saying what things there are. They are saying what things are. And yet they freely deploy negative concepts like not-material in doing all that. My claim, again, is not that the Chart Ontology is true. Rather, I claim only that it is coherent, and that its proponents are plainly engaged in categorial ontology.

I conclude, then, that there is no requirement – whether in sound thinking or in the abstruse art of ontological categorizing – to deploy only positive concepts. The Positive Requirement fails, and so too does the spirit concept argument.

Before moving on, let me point out what has happened here. We began our study by identifying an important question about human nature – the category question. To ask that question is to take part in the grand tradition of ontological categorizing. And it is from that very activity that I have found an objection to the spirit concept argument. I conclude from this, not just that the spirit concept argument is unsound, but that it fits poorly within any philosophical worldview with room for inquiry into human nature in the first place.

My criticism of the spirit concept argument may be extended; we now have the resources to appreciate another problem. According to the third premise, there is a key link between what concepts we have and what is possible. It says, recall: If thinking matter is possible, it is not the case that we have a distinct positive concept of God's being a divine spirit.

Let's call this Key Link. There are plenty of complaints one might direct against Key Link. There may be, for example, no general bridge between our conceptual resources and modality (perhaps reality is not so respectful of our concepts as we might wish). But I do not propose to advance that kind of objection. Instead, I'll show how the reply I've developed to the Positive Requirement applies here with equal force. So even if the Positive Requirement could be shored up to avoid my criticism, the spirit concept argument would nonetheless be vulnerable to attack.

Before criticizing Key Link, let me offer a word on its behalf in the form of a brief speech, which will express Moreland's basic case for Key Link:

Begin with a general principle. Reality is unmixed in this sense: if what it is to be a thing of a certain real kind is to be such-and-such, then what it is to be a thing of some distinct real kind does not involve such-and-such. The reason is simple: since these kinds are indeed distinct, their specific natures must be distinct as well. Accordingly, the concepts by which we specify real kinds must not themselves be mixed. The principle may be applied to our concepts of the (alleged) kinds *thinking matter* and *spirit*. If we indeed have these concepts then they are distinct and unmixed. But the concepts of thinking matter and spirit are mixed – to be a spirit is to be a thinking thing and to be thinking matter is to be a thinking thing. The very concept (and thus the possibility) of either thinking matter or of a spirit must, then, be defective. So, if one is possible and conceptually aboveboard, the other is not. Accordingly, if thinking matter is possible and conceptually aboveboard, then spirits are not and we do not, after all, have an adequate concept of a spirit.

There is something appealing about the basic idea here, I think. If some kinds are indeed real (not made-up or gerrymandered) and distinct, then they must have distinct natures. The aforementioned speech proposes that the distinctness at hand must involve non-overlap. This non-overlap condition is the core of Moreland's case for Key Link. Here's how he puts it:

> By claiming that thinking matter is possible [as the materialist does], it follows that the various mental properties of consciousness – sensation, other forms of awareness, thought, belief, desire, volitional choices done for the sake of ends–could characterize material substances. If this is so, then granting the reality of immaterial spirits for the sake of argument, one cannot use mental properties to characterize the nature of a spirit, since those properties are consistent with both a spirit and a material substance.[19]

I demur. We can use mental concepts to characterize the nature of a spirit, even if those properties could be had by both material and immaterial beings. Indeed, we can do so in our most serious and metaphysical moods, even when doing old-fashioned categorial ontology. To demonstrate this, I need only point again to the Chart Ontology. Can the Chart ontologist say what it is to be a material thinking thing? With ease. Recall that, according to the Chart ontologist (and categorial ontologists in general), saying what something is involves pointing to a node within the chart. To say what a spirit is, then, the Chart ontologist need only point to the proper node in the chart (in this case, the thinking immaterial thing node). To be a spirit is to fall within that node in the grand hierarchy of being; it is to be a thinking material concretum. That mental properties characterize spirits as well as material thinking things is no more a problem than that

---

[19] Moreland (2013, pp. 39–40).

immateriality characterizes both some abstracta (numbers, say) and some concreta (God and demons, say).

Here's where we're at. I have examined two arguments for dualism that begin with assumptions that have special attraction to the monotheist. I have contended that those arguments fail. But we are not yet in a position to dispatch our opening suspicion that monotheism supports or suggests or otherwise is conducive toward dualism. For other arguments remain in the dualist's arsenal. Such are the subject of the next section.

3 Simplicity and Mystery

3.1 From Simplicity to Dualism

It is sometimes said that God is an ontological dangler – an extra bit that offends Ockham's Razor. Simplicity, the idea goes, recommends that we slice off the dangler, withhold belief in the Almighty – and in anything like God at all, really – in favor of a less profligate naturalism. Reality is a desert landscape, exhausted by and rooted within nature and nature alone. The merits and demerits of this approach are well-known and I will not recite them here.

But I want to now consider a less well-known argument that begins along similar lines – with the conviction that simpler is better – that, in a somewhat ironic twist, supports dualism.[20] This argument begins with the observation that the monotheistic materialist, unlike the monotheistic dualist, is committed to an unattractive theoretical complexity. To see why, consider this matrix:

	Thinking	**Not-thinking**
Wholly material		
Not-wholly material		

Metaphysical theories differ over which boxes are filled or unfilled. According to one form of radical eliminative materialism, for example, only the upper-right-hand box is filled; there are only material things, and none of them think. Ontological nihilists say no boxes are filled.

One-box or no-box theories are attractively simple. Of course, one shouldn't, on that basis alone, insist on a one-box or no-box theory. Any reason to think that a box is filled counts against theories according to which it isn't. If you've ever seen a rock (an unthinking material being), for example, you've acquired

---

[20] The arguments of this section simplify and update those given in Bailey (2020a).

some evidence against any no-box theory. Simplicity isn't everything. But it is one important factor to be weighed in theory choice. Unfilled boxes confer simplicity benefits on a theory. Filled boxes incur complexity costs.

We may use this framework to build a case against the conjunction of monotheism and materialism. The monotheistic materialist says that at least two boxes are filled: immaterial things that think (God), and wholly material things that think (us). The dualist, by contrast, need only affirm that one box is filled: immaterial things that think (God and us). The dualist monotheist therefore enjoys an important and categorical simplicity advantage over the materialist. Put a little differently: if we can get away with fewer filled boxes, we should. We can get by with fewer filled boxes. So we should. And we, by monotheism, already know a bit about which boxes are filled – we know that at least one thinking thing, God, is wholly immaterial – so let's fill that box and be done with it. There's just no need to posit anything at all in that pesky upper-left-hand box.

There's something to this argument. It uncovers a theoretical advantage monotheistic dualism enjoys over monotheistic materialism. I do not think the argument is dispositive, though.

First, the simplicity advantage that accrues to dualism is minimal. If we switch the matrix used to measure simplicity, we're in a position to see why:

	Thinking	**Not-thinking**
Embodied		
Not-embodied		

The dualist and the materialist will agree that *both* left-hand boxes are to be filled. For we are embodied thinking things. Even if we aren't our bodies, we still *have* bodies. And God is a non-embodied thinking thing. God has no body. There is no difference here between dualists and materialists. And so there is no simplicity difference. This little matrix switch shows that simplicity considerations are sensitive to framing. What one wants here is an *argument* that the first matrix (as opposed to, or in addition to the second) is an appropriate measure of theoretical complexity or simplicity. Absent such an argument, dualism's simplicity advantage is not strong.

Second, it is unclear that counting filled boxes is a good way to measure theoretical complexity. Here is an alternative: count, not filled boxes, but filled rows or columns. What we're trying to measure here is *categorical* complexity: how many *kinds* of things a metaphysical theory affirms. Filled boxes indicate *intersections* of categories affirmed by a theory. But it is the categories themselves – filled rows or columns – that indicate complexity. If this is correct, then monotheistic dualism and monotheistic materialism are closer to being on a par. They both affirm that the "thinking" column is filled in both matrices. Dualists who think that there are wholly material beings or that we are embodied, furthermore, will agree with the materialist that both the "wholly material" and "embodied" rows are filled. The only kind of dualist who can claim victory here over the materialist is one who denies that there are wholly material objects at all (a certain kind of radical idealist, say); according to this sort of theory, both the "wholly material" and "embodied" rows are unfilled. There is something attractive about radical idealism.[21] But it's not for everyone; I'd wager that most monotheistic dualists think that we have bodies and that there are wholly material beings. I conclude, then, that most dualists cannot help themselves to this style of argument.

Third, there are monotheistic reasons to doubt that theoretical simplicity indicates truth, especially when measured by unfilled rows, columns, or boxes. Monotheists believe that there is an almighty and creative God. Many say that God takes pleasure in the sheer variety of creation. With a God like *that* on the loose, a desert landscape is not quite what one should expect. One should expect, instead, a verdant rainforest. A creative and powerful God interested in bringing variety into being – in seeing to it that all sorts of possibilities are actual – might well fill all manner of boxes, simplicity be damned. Indeed, on this plenitudinous vision of monotheism, simplicity arguments like the one considered here get things exactly backwards. So long as these boxes *can* be filled, there is some reason to think they are.

The caveat – so long as they *can* be filled – is important. The monotheistic case for plenitude given here succeeds only if it is indeed possible for a wholly material being to think. So let us now turn to another classic argument for dualism concerning that very possibility.

3.2 Impossibility

Can material objects think? A negative answer would be bad news for materialism. So Alvin Plantinga: "no material objects can think . . . But of course I can think; therefore I am not a material object." Fair enough. But what reason is there to think that no material object can think? In answer to that question, consider this classic thought experiment from G. W. Leibniz:

> It must be confessed, moreover, that perception, and that which depends on it, are inexplicable by mechanical causes, that is by figures and motions. And supposing there were a machine so constructed as to think, feel and have

---

[21] Segal & Goldschmidt (2017).

perception, we could conceive of it as enlarged and yet preserving the same proportions, so that we might enter it as into a mill. And this granted, we should only find on visiting it, pieces which push one against another, but never anything by which to explain a perception.[22]

Leibniz's point is that there can be no full and purely mechanistic explanation of thinking. Step inside a thinking machine, and all you'll find is various parts pushing and pulling, all without any explanation of thought. Leibniz's point is especially potent when applied to instances of *phenomenal consciousness* – thoughts where there is *something it is like* to have them, such as vivid sensory experiences or pains.[23] Even if we might find in the thinking machine a satisfying mechanistic explanation for the machine's belief that two and two is four, there can be no such explanation for the machine's being in pain. The point extends beyond simple mechanistic explanations. Other kinds of physical interaction – gravity, electromagnetism, and so on – cannot explain thought either. But were materialism true, there would have to be such an explanation. Absent one, it would be entirely mysterious – indeed, seemingly impossible – that a material thing could think.

This impossibility argument has seemed potent to many. Materialists had better have a good reply.

3.3 Magic

And they do.

A phenomenon is *magical*, let us say, to the degree that it is modally and explanatorily independent of the material world. Magic comes in degrees. *Pure* magic swings entirely free of the material world.[24] But of course, there might be less pure forms of magic too – phenomena that depend only in part on, or are only explained in part by, the material world. To be clear, I don't use "magical" as a term of abuse. For one, monotheists like me believe in magic in the sense at hand. All sorts of facts about God are, to some degree, modally and explanatorily independent of the material world: they can obtain without a material world at all, and are not explained in any way by laws of nature or the activity of electrons or ion channels or gravitational waves or what have you.

Consider now God's thought that the sum of two and two is four. Or God's decision to create the cosmos. Or the pleasure God takes in pure cogitation. These would appear to be instances of mentality. I shall suppose they are. These would also appear to be instances of pure magic. If that's right – and I shall

---

[22] *Monadology* 17; this translation appears in Leibniz (1951, p. 536).   [23] Block (1995, p. 230).

[24] To make things more precise, we could identify various flavors of modal and explanatory relations that might tether the mental to the physical. For a good start, see Rasmussen (2018, p. 335) on *basic mentality*. *Pure* magic involves basic mentality in all three of Rasmussen's senses.

suppose it is – then the monotheist is committed, not just to the possibility of magic in general, but to the possibility of *pure magical thinking*. There is, as it were, no *how* to these thoughts of God's. They are not to be accounted for by the firing of neurons or the electromagnetic properties of particles, or anything like that at all. If you ask "*how* does God manage to think?," hoping for a mechanistic or material explanation, you will be frustrated. No such explanation is forthcoming. The monotheist, furthermore, embraces this magical thinking with open arms. The independence of God's mentality from the material not an unwelcome or costly consequence to be hidden away or discounted.

Theism invites a magical answer to the mentality question, a magical theory of mind. And this theory undercuts the impossibility argument. Here's why. Leibniz and Plantinga and many others have wanted to know *how* a composite material object could manage to think; is it by pushing, or pulling, or what? *How does it all work?*

There is no *how.* We are wholly material beings, to be sure, and in exactly the sense we have been discussing. We are made only of unthinking items treated by fundamental physics; if you made a list of all our parts, no soul or ghost or spirit would appear on it. But our thinking is magical. It is modally and explanatorily independent of the material world. Our thinking does not succumb to explanation in terms of the workings of the material world. It cannot be explained by the motions or shapes or charges of particles. Or fields. Or gravitational waves. Or anything like that at all. It is magic. There is no how.

This is a mysterious view. Of course it is. It is inevitable that some will scoff. The naturalist – who maintains that there is no magic, and that magical theories are off-limits or otherwise intellectually naughty – will scoff for familiar reasons. But my arguments here aren't addressed to naturalists. I instead address those of my fellow monotheists who would heap scorn on magical thinking. The monotheist I imagine here will insist that thinking demands an explanation, and that the answer given here – that thinking could be magical – incurs a grave theoretical cost.

This retort is almost irresistible. And yet, it is wrong. For the monotheist, magical thinking is a mystery already accepted. The theoretical costs accrued by its mysteriousness have, if you like, *already been priced in.* For God's thinking is magical. It is already possible, *by the monotheist's own lights*, that something should think even though its thoughts are not to be accounted for by the workings of the material world. So though the claim that magical thinking incurs some grave theoretical cost may be a strike against monotheism, it is not, *given monotheism*, a strike against materialism.

The upshot is that the monotheistic materialist has an interesting and dialectically potent reply to the impossibility argument. That argument presupposes that, if we are wholly material, there must be some explanation of our thinking in terms of the workings of the material world. It is open to the monotheistic materialist to reply that our thought is like God's – magical and therefore not explained by or modally tethered to the workings of the material world.

3.4 Mystery

Given monotheism, the impossibility argument doesn't succeed. But it does suggest another argument for dualism. To understand that argument, it's helpful to first consider an important reply to the impossibility argument by a monotheistic materialist.

According to Peter van Inwagen, dualists and materialists stand in parity. What Leibniz' thought experiment shows us is that *thinking* is mysterious – apparently impossible – not the hypothesis that a *material* being thinks. For it is equally mysterious – apparently impossible – that an *immaterial* being should think.[25] Since this is a problem that equally plagues both dualists and materialists, it is no reason to reject materialism.

Even if van Inwagen is correct – if it is mysterious, apparently impossible – that an *im*material being should think, materialism isn't yet off the hook. For Leibniz's insight can still be used in an argument for dualism that has special force given monotheism.

That argument unfolds as follows. An important dimension of theory choice is the multiplication, not of entities, but of *mysteries*. Positing more mysteries – things that sure look impossible – than is necessary is a theoretical vice. On the assumption of monotheism, dualism has an important advantage here. The dualist affirms just one mystery – that immaterial things can think (God and us). But the materialist affirms *two*: both that immaterial things can think (God), and that material things can think as well (us). Two mysteries are worse than one. Point to the dualist.[26]

The argument can be strengthened. The deepest mystery here is that something could think *by way of the activity of its parts*. That is the mystery materialists must affirm and that dualists deny. It is a price that the materialist must pay and that the dualist need not. Or so say the critics of materialism. Thus Plantinga:

> "How does an electron manage to have a charge?" is an improper question.
> There's no how to it … The same is true of a self and thinking: it's not done
> by underlying activity or workings; it's a basic and immediate activity of the

---

[25] van Inwagen (2015, p. 235).

[26] So Plantinga (2007, p. 120): "suppose we take … theism seriously. Then we are already committed to the existence of a thinking immaterial being: God himself … The appearance of impossibility in an immaterial object's thinking, if there were such an appearance, would therefore be an illusion."

self. But then the important difference, here, between materialism and immaterialism is that if a material thing managed to think, it would have to be by way of the activity of its parts.[27]

Point, again, to the dualist; or so the mystery argument goes.

In reply, I'll contend that the monotheistic materialist has some interesting and dialectically potent resources with which to resist. In fact, I'll show that, on monotheism, a version of the mystery argument can be turned into a case *for* materialism.

Dualists who would press the mystery argument face a dilemma. Our thinking is either magical on their view, or it is not. If it is magical, then the dualist can hardly complain when the materialist resorts to magic as well. If it is not magical, then the materialist may appropriate the very explanatory or modal relations that the dualist herself countenances (tethering our thinking and the activity of the material world). In neither case does the materialist invoke more or deeper mystery than does the dualist. So in neither case does the mystery argument succeed as an argument for dualism over materialism.

That's my reply in a nutshell. I'll now work through the dilemma's horns more carefully.

Let us suppose that dualism is true, and that the thinking of human beings is magical. We think, to be sure. But we do not think by way of the activity of the parts of our bodies. There is, rather, no how to things.

The mystery argument attempts to saddle the materialist with a mystery: that material things think by way of the activity of their parts. The magical reply is by now familiar. It goes like this: No; material things like us can think, to be sure, but there is no how to it. Our thinking is, as the dualist says, magical.

The magical dualist here under consideration cannot consistently reply that magical thinking is bad or implausible or otherwise intellectually off-limits. Magical thinking is a component of her own view. For dualism to enjoy a dialectical advantage here, there would have to be an asymmetry between these two theses:

> **Soul Magic**: people (who are *not* wholly material) think, but not in any sense by way of the activity of the parts of their bodies. You have a brain, sure; but in no sense at all is your thinking modally or explanatorily tethered to that brain or the activity of its parts. Your thinking is, instead, magical.
>
> **Body Magic**: people (who *are* wholly material) think, but not in any sense by way of the activity of the parts of their bodies. You have a brain, sure; but

---

[27] Plantinga (2007, p. 117).

in no sense at all is your thinking modally or explanatorily tethered to that brain or the activity of its parts. Your thinking is, instead, magical.

I propose that Soul Magic and Body Magic – mysterious though they may be – are on a par when it comes to mystery. Perhaps they are quite badly off here, so badly off as to not even count as theories. But they are in this respect the same. *Both*, I think, have a sheen of apparent impossibility or puzzlingness. Given this symmetry, there is no argument here for dualism against materialism.

Some dualists sound like they affirm a magical view of thinking, that there's no *how* to things when it comes to thinking of an immaterial self or soul. They sound like they opt for the first horn of my dilemma. But there is another horn to consider. Perhaps dualism is true, but our thinking is still modally or explanatorily tethered to the material. In another context, Plantinga correctly notes: "Localization studies show that when certain kinds of mental activity occur, certain parts of the brain display increased blood flow and increased electrical activity . . . mental activity is also in a certain important way *dependent* on brain activity and brain condition."[28]

Plantinga is not alone here. A common refrain among contemporary dualists is that their view is fully compatible with the apparent truth that the activity of our minds is somehow generated by the activity of various parts within our bodies (and in particular, our brains). A few quick examples demonstrate the point. So E. J. Lowe:

> In these terms, then, the dualist may be construed as holding that a person is not to be identified with his or her body, nor with any part of it, such as the brain. On this view, a *person – not* the person's body or brain – feels pain and has desires, even if it is true to say that a person feels pain or has desires *only because* his or her body or brain is in a certain physical state.[29]

Charles Taliferro:

> I not only sense and perceive, but think and form judgments *with my brain*, not in the sense that my brain is a mere tool in these activities.[30]

William Hasker:

> On the other hand, the commissurotomy and multiple personality evidence, along with much, much else, strongly suggests that the *source* of conscious experience is to be found in the brain and nervous system . . . And there is a great deal more evidence that shows the role of the brain in *generating* conscious experiences of various sorts.[31]

---

[28] Plantinga (2006, p. 22), emphasis original. [29] Lowe (2010, p. 441), emphasis original.
[30] Taliaferro (1997, p. 117), emphasis added. [31] Hasker (2010, pp. 183–84), emphasis added.

J. P. Moreland:

> Consider, for example, the discovery that if one's mirror neurons are damaged, then one cannot feel empathy for another. How are we to explain this? ... [on] substance dualism, a feeling of empathy is an irreducible state of consciousness in the soul whose obtaining *depends (while embodied) on the firing of mirror neurons.*[32]

Eric LaRock and Robin Collins:

> Moreover, most contemporary dualists hold to a naturalistic approach [on which] ... the human soul derives certain properties from the human brain ... very few, if any, noteworthy dualists have denied that "soul" *causally depends in a very detailed way* on the physical.[33]

The dualists I've quoted differ in their vocabulary, but they all seem to affirm that *some* dependence relation holds between mind and body (and in particular, the brain). The relation may be contingent. It may only be one of efficient causation. It may be strictly limited to cases involving embodied human persons. And it may carry only a partial rather than a full explanation, as when the activity of a brain *contributes to* or *helps* generate thinking activity in a soul. But it holds nonetheless. Our thinking is not magical; it is tethered.

I'll put the second horn of my dilemma as this claim:

> **Tethered Soul:** when an embodied human person (who is an immaterial soul) thinks, it is at least partly because the parts of her body are in a certain physical state.

The idea here is simple. When you think, it's at least partly a result of (partly rooted in, partly grounded by, a contingent consequence of, etc.) activity in your body. Our thinking is not pure magic. It is at least partly tethered. Thus tethered dualism.

I'll now advance two materialist-friendly replies. The first will rebut the mystery argument by appropriating the central insight of tethered dualism. The second will suggest a turn of that argument that supports materialism over dualism.

First: an *appropriation*. It is open to the materialist to affirm a thesis *very much like* Tethered Soul, and so to eschew pure magic, just like the tethered dualist:

---

[32] Moreland (2018, p. 107), emphasis added.
[33] LaRock & Collins (2016, pp. 138–40), emphasis added. See also Collins (2011, pp. 233–35).

Tethered Body: when a human person (who is a wholly material being) thinks, it is at least partly because her parts are in a certain physical state.[34]

The materialist opting for Tethered Body may appropriate anything the dualist says on behalf of Tethered Soul. If Tethered Soul successfully captures the sense in which our thought is not magical, so too does Tethered Body. If Tethered Soul is sufficiently robust as to count as a genuine theory and not mere mystery-mongering (unlike Soul Magic and Body Magic say), then so too is Tethered Body. Tethered Soul and Body have the same theoretical virtues. And if Tethered Body has any theoretical vices – trading in mystery, for example – so too does Tethered Soul. Affirming Tethered Body, then, incurs no extra theoretical cost to the materialist. The mystery of Tethered Soul is no better than the mystery of Tethered Body. So reflection on these theses provides no argument for dualism against materialism.

Second: a *turn*. Tethered Body enjoys a significant advantage over Tethered Soul, a result that both undermines the mystery argument and supports materialism over dualism.

According to tethered dualists, you think at least partly because some things *disjoint* from you have certain physical properties. Somehow, though the parts of your body are not parts of you, your mental life is generated by the activity of those items. That thought should come into being this way – leaping across the divide from body to soul, as it were – is a great mystery. Dualists who affirm Tethered Soul take on a cost.

We can illustrate with a variation on Leibniz's thought experiment. Step inside a huge and complicated contraption. Pulleys, levers, cogs, and spinning wheels surround you. It is a wonder to behold and would fill the heart of any machinist with delight. But the hypothesis that these mechanical workings could explain the thought of the machine as a whole is incredible. Now consider a second hypothesis: something *else* thinks because of those mechanical workings – some immaterial item that shares no parts at all with the machine. The first hypothesis is incredible. That is Leibniz's point. The second is *more* incredible. It has all the mystery of the first hypothesis and more to spare. For it says that activity of some physical items can explain, not the thinking of the machine, but something that doesn't even overlap the machine.

I do not claim that the revised thought experiment is a knockdown argument against dualism. It isn't. Nor do I claim that it is always bad to posit some immaterial thinking thing, as the second hypothesis does. Whatever theoretical

---

[34] *Union* dualists who think we are partly material and partly immaterial (composed of body and soul, say) can affirm Tethered Body and are not my target here. For objections to union dualism, see Bailey (2015, pp. 168–70).

costs to such have already been priced in for the theist, after all. Rather, adding that a soul's thinking is tethered to and explained in any way by the activity of a body incurs an additional theoretical cost. It is the extra *tie* here that is the problem, not the soul as such.

The cost of affirming Tethered Body alone, I submit, is comparatively modest. For Tethered Body does not require that any explanation or tethering tie can make the leap from the parts of one thing – a body – to another thing altogether – a soul. It says, instead, that the tethering tie binds the properties of a thing's parts to the thing itself. That something could think because its own parts have certain physical properties strains credulity at least a little. I grant this. But that something could think because the parts of something *else* have certain physical properties strains credulity even more.

It is mysterious indeed how Tethered Body could be true. Materialists may well be stuck with that mystery. Too bad for materialists. Dualists opting for the second horn, however, are stuck with Tethered Soul – and that is worse. I conclude that tethered dualists don't have a case against materialism in the mystery argument. Indeed, by their very own lights, that argument reveals a weakness in dualism and a relative strength in materialism.

Since the mystery argument does not support dualism over materialism in the case of either horn of my dilemma, I conclude that the argument does not succeed at all.

3.5 The Nagging Suspicion and Divine Thinking

Let's take stock. I have, so far, considered a range of arguments for dualism. Each is an attempt to make good on the nagging suspicion that monotheists, by virtue of rejecting naturalism, should exhibit a natural affinity to dualism. The arguments do not succeed.

There is something to the nagging suspicion, of course. Some popular slogans in the metaphysics of mind and human persons – answers to the category, modal, or mentality questions, that is – simply won't do for the monotheist. Three examples will illustrate:

First, it is possible that a wholly immaterial being thinks. Thinking is not reserved only for, say, wholly material or partly material creatures. Arguments for materialist answers to the category question from the slogan that only material beings exist or can think (because thinking requires a brain, say, or because the concept of an immaterial being is incoherent)[35] are non-starters for the monotheist. One easy route to a materialist answer to the category question is closed.

---

[35] Carruthers (2004, pp. 152–53).

Second, no identity theory will do. Identity theories of the kind I have in mind maintain that, for every mental property or state, there is a physical property or state to which it is identical.[36] These identity theories answer the mentality question; they say how the physical properties of our bodies relate to our mental properties – by *being* them in a full and strict sense. They do this by appealing to the more general claim that every mental property is a physical property. The monotheist must reject such theories, for God has mental properties or states and exhibits no physical properties or states at all.

Third, it is possible for a wholly immaterial being to causally interact with the material world. This follows, at least, if God's creative activity in making the cosmos involves causal interaction. And it would certainly appear to. There are many ways things can causally interact: kissing, punching, stretching, pushing, and so on. Making, as when God called the cosmos into being some thirteen billion years ago, falls among such interactions. Making is a kind of causal relation.[37] Arguments for materialism according to which only material things can interact with the material world are also non-starters. Another easy route to the materialist answer to the category question, then, is closed.

Here's the upshot. A fairly minimal monotheistic hypothesis – suitably supplemented with the assumption of divine thinking – is incompatible with a variety of popular arguments or slogans in the metaphysics of human nature that are broadly naturalistic. They encapsulate various flavors and dimensions of naturalism. But for the monotheist, they just won't do.

So there is *something* to the nagging suspicion. But the arguments considered that take us to full-blown dualism do not succeed.

Throughout, I've made generous use of a substantive assumption of divine mentality. I have assumed that God thinks. It is now time to subject this assumption to some well-deserved scrutiny. For as we'll see in the next section, some classical expositions of the *uniqueness* of God call into question that critical assumption or the way in which it's been deployed so far. On those views, God is so unique that God is unlike anything else, which really puts a spanner in the works of anyone who'd reason from God's nature to ours.

4 God Alone

4.1 Divine Thinking Revisited

We have observed that, if there really is one almighty God, and if that God does indeed think – a widely accepted auxiliary assumption – then some initially

---

[36] Place (1956); Smart (1959).

[37] In addition to initially *making* the cosmos, many say that God also *sustains* it in an ongoing way. For helpful treatment of the distinction, see Segal (forthcoming).

compelling arguments for dualism crumble. In the midst of that controlled demolition, we saw a novel and positive case for an odd form of materialism. God's magical thinking invites the idea that our thinking is magical too – despite our being wholly material beings.

It is time to now examine more closely the auxiliary assumption of divine thinking and its role in arguments that would take us from the divine nature to our own. I'll begin by presenting two pictures or explications of the uniqueness of God, one of which challenges the way we've been using the hypothesis of divine thought. I'll then draw out the consequences that follow. In short: views that emphasize the absolute uniqueness of God – as when God's uniqueness precludes God's sharing any category at all with other things – impose a serious challenge to reasoning from God's nature to our own.

4.2 Picture Thinking

Divine uniqueness is common to the great Abrahamic traditions of Judaism, Christianity, and Islam. So the Shahada ("There is no god but God … "), the Nicene Creed ("We believe in one God, the Father Almighty"), and the Shema Yisrael (" … the LORD our God, the LORD is one … ").

Tradition is clear; God is one. But what does it mean, exactly, to say that God is one or that there is only one God? In what ways is God unique or alone?

These questions, as we'll see, impinge on arguments that would take us from premises about God's nature to conclusions about our own. But note that they are of wider import too. God is, Abrahamic monotheists agree, a supremely deserving object of worship. Of course many things rightly command our attention, respect, and even love: family, school, country, friends, and more besides. But the attention, respect, adoration, love, duty – in a word, regard – that we owe God surpasses all else. If God truly deserves this unsurpassed regard, God must be special indeed – set apart from and elevated above all else. The uniqueness of God is one tool the Abrahamic philosophical theologian may deploy in limning that divine elevation. To learn how God is unique is to learn how or why God rightly commands our regard.

We will now consider two approaches to the uniqueness of God, beginning with some picture-thinking that informs them.

Imagine, then, a special cupboard filled with dishes and cups of diverse shapes and sizes and hues. And imagine you're in search of a great and singular treasure, unsurpassed in worth and to be prized above all else. How might one use this image – a cabinet and a search for unsurpassed treasure – to think about the uniqueness of God?

Here is one way:

Counting

Select some criterion for being a great and singular treasure – some special combination of beauty and function and color, for example. With a tally counter in hand and that criterion in mind, peer into the cupboard and make an inventory of all its contents. Each time you encounter a being that meets the criterion, click. By the time you're done, you'll have clicked once and only once – perhaps when examining a lovely blue cup. For the treasure to be unique in the target sense is for one and only one thing in the cabinet to meet the criterion.

And here is another:

Difference

Open the pantry of reality and make an inventory of all things visible and invisible. Try as you might, you'll not find a great and singular treasure in that cupboard. The conclusion to draw here is not there is no treasure. One must, instead, inquire into the cupboard itself. And here's what you'll find. The cupboard is unlike its contents (lovely though they may be, they're just dishes and cups). It is different from them and utterly singular: not one dish among many, but rather that on which all dishes rest. The cabinet is the treasure. For the treasure to be unique is for it to be different from all the dishes and cups and so not counted among them.

These are rough and imperfect images. But they can help us come to initial grips with two approaches to the uniqueness of God. Let's translate the images into more literal statements of philosophical theology.

On one approach – the way of counting – God is an item within the great pantry of reality. If you made a list of all beings visible and invisible, God would show up on that list, and God would be unique or singular or one because, of all the items on the list, God alone had the qualifying feature for godhood – some special combination of knowledge, power, and goodness, for example. As a slogan: God is unique because the number of gods – divine beings blessed with sufficient knowledge, power, and goodness, say – is precisely one.

Perhaps the main thing to be said on behalf of the way of counting is that it makes plain sense of the uniqueness of God. It gives a strict and straightforward meaning to the word "one" in statements like "God is one." The meaning is this: *one in number*. We know what it is for things to be one (or three, or seven) in number. Figuring out *that* is as easy as counting to one (or three, or seven). There may be puzzles and difficulties in zeroing in on an appropriate criterion of divinity, of course, but any trouble lies more in "God" than in "one." And so we know what it means to say that God is one.

On the second approach – the way of difference – God is not an item within the special cupboard at all. Perhaps pagan idols can be counted in this way, but not the Almighty. If you made a list of all beings visible and invisible, God would not show up on that list. For God is not just another being. God is, rather, that on which all beings depend, and within which they live and move. As a somewhat cryptic slogan: God is unique because God is wholly other. As a slightly less cryptic slogan: God is unique because God is wholly different from everything else.

Perhaps the main thing to be said on behalf of the way of difference is that it pays due respect to the distinction between creator (God) and creation (everything else). A defining feature of monotheism – what sets it apart from mere theism and other less ambitious rejections of naturalism – is that it affirms a vast divide between God and all other things. Affirming that divide is not only pious. It also fits well with metaphysical roles God has been thought to play – being the ground of being or even Being itself. One need not pretend to know what all this means – what it is for something to be Being itself, for example – to see that the way of difference is at least an *attempt* to give God due metaphysical distinction.

I'll now give special attention to the way of difference and its connections to our study of human nature.

4.3 Difference and Category

Great thinkers across the Abrahamic traditions have begun their study of the uniqueness of God with the slogan *God is One*. We can do no better. This Element is not primarily an exercise in historical philosophy or theology. But a few representative samples from the distant past will help get things started.

Maimonides writes:

> [T]his One, Who is the cause of [the existence of] everything, is one. His oneness is unlike the oneness of a genus, or of a species. Nor is it like the oneness of a single composed individual, which can be divided into many units. Nor is His oneness like that of the simple body which is one in number but infinitely divisible. Rather He, may He be exalted, is one with a oneness for which there is no comparison at all.[38]

This is a rich passage, and we cannot do it full justice here. But for now, notice: God is one, and not – in any sense at all, it seems – many. God is absolutely simple: without either actual or even potential division. And that divine

---

[38] Maimonides (1974, p.74).

oneness – the way in which God is one – is itself unique and not enjoyed by any other items. God is unique, and the way in which God is unique is itself unique.

In a similar spirit, Al-Ghazali says:

> [T]he Creator most high is one, meaning that he is not quantifiable, meaning that quantification denies something's wholeness by dividing it. But [God] is not divisible, since divisibility pertains to things that are quantifiable. Quantification results in division into parts, becoming smaller. But that which is not quantifiable cannot be described as divisible.[39]

Ghazali claims that God's oneness is not just a matter of being countable by a certain number (the number one, for example). Rather, God is beyond counting altogether, because God is absolutely simple. Somehow quantification of any kind implies divisibility, and so the simplicity of God demands that though God is one, there is not one God.

I've quoted a medieval Jewish philosopher and medieval Islamic philosopher; it's only fair to attend now to a medieval Christian voice. So St. Thomas Aquinas:

> God is one . . . For it is manifest that the reason why any singular thing is "this particular thing" is because it cannot be communicated to many . . . Now this belongs to God alone; for God Himself is His own nature, as was shown above. Therefore, in the very same way God is God, and He is this God. Impossible is it therefore that many Gods should exist.[40]

Thomas moves from the oneness of God to denying that there are many gods. And the reason given for this connection is simple: were there many gods, there would be many items each sharing a nature. But the divine nature is identical to God – there's divine simplicity again – and so cannot be shared. Elsewhere, Thomas extends the thought in this way:

> [S]ince the existence of God is His essence, if God were in any genus, He would be the genus "being," because, since genus is predicated as an essential it refers to the essence of a thing. But the Philosopher has shown that being cannot be a genus, for every genus has differences distinct from its generic essence. Now no difference can exist distinct from being; for non-being cannot be a difference. It follows then that God is not in a genus.[41]

---

[39] Al-Ghazali (2005, p. 199). Ghazali goes on to say that "Furthermore, [one] can be understood as that which has no equal in its rank, such as when we say that the sun is one. In this sense also the Creator most high is one, since he has no peer" – but this suggests a rather different theory of the uniqueness of God, one I'll touch on in the next section.

[40] Aquinas (1947, Ia, q. 11, a.3).   [41] Aquinas (1947, Ia, q. 3, a.5).

The claim here is that God does not even share the most general genus of all (being) with other things. Uniqueness requires that God shares *no ontological category at all* with any being.

There is much more to say about these passages, and other rich passages we'd do well to consult besides. But we shall have to content ourselves with this stale summary: a storied cluster of thinkers across Abrahamic traditions are keen to explain God's uniqueness. Though there are certainly differences and peculiarities, all appeal to some combination of the following theses: God is absolutely simple. And on account of that absolute simplicity, God is therefore beyond any shared category with any other item. Indeed, God is beyond categories altogether, and so God's oneness does not lie in the fact that God alone falls under a given kind. God's uniqueness does not lie in God being the one and only one (one in number, that is) item that satisfies some criterion of divinity. It lies in being fundamentally different from all other things.[42]

Pictures do not do the view justice, but two more charts may help us better understand the ways of counting and difference. A proponent of the way of counting might deploy something like Figure 2.

Think of "perfect" here as shorthand for some suitable combination of properties like omniscience, omnipotence, and omnibenevolence. After drawing a chart like Figure 2, the proponent of the way of counting points to the "perfect thinking immaterial object" node and observes that exactly one item falls within it.[43] That item is the one true God. Were (*per impossibile*) two items to fall under that category, of course, monotheism wouldn't be true, since God wouldn't be unique; some form of polytheism, instead, would be true.

The proponent of the way of difference thinks this is all nonsense, and perhaps even harmful nonsense. For it suggests that God lies *within* something else, nested inside one of reality's many layers or categories. The proponent of the way of difference would instead favor a chart like Figure 3.

On the way of looking at things expressed in Figure 3, God is not a concrete object among other concrete objects, or even a perfect being among imperfect beings. God isn't even a thing among things. God is separate, apart, wholly different.

---

[42] The views I've given the "counting" and "difference" labels map approximately onto "theistic personalism" and "classical theism." See Davies (2004, pp. 2–15). I'm avoiding Davies' terms for two reasons: they seem tendentious, and they're bound up with questions about divine simplicity, whether God is a person, theological predication, and more – all beyond the scope of the present study and whether God shares any categories with other beings. For more on classical theism and its controversies, see Burns (2015).

[43] So Oppy (2014, p. 1): "to be God is just to be the one and only god, where to be a god is to be a superhuman being or entity who has and exercises power over the natural world." See also Tuggy (2017).

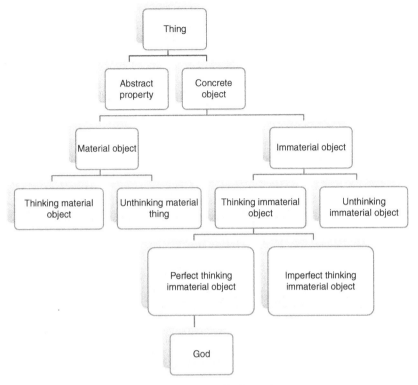

Figure 2 A categorical ontology

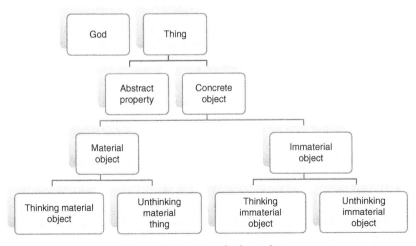

Figure 3 A categorical ontology

And it has to be like this, given the assumptions common to thinkers like Maimonides, al-Ghazali, or Thomas. Consider the following modification, for example, as seen in Figure 4.

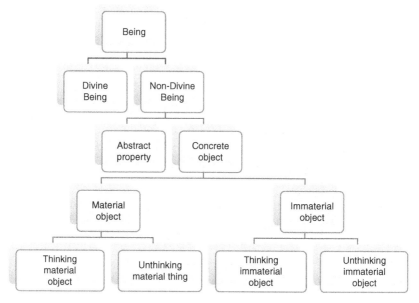

Figure 4 A categorical ontology

You might have thought that a chart like Figure 4 could pay due respect to the uniqueness of God. God stands alone within the category of *divine being*; all else lies within *non-divine being*. But, according to Aquinas, this will not do. First, there is no fully general genus or category of being in the first place (for there are no non-beings, and so no complement to *being*). And other arguments in the tradition purport to show that, even if there were such a fully general category, to place God within it alongside others would involve *differentiation* – from other beings, that is – and thus unacceptable *limits* on the divine nature. Thus Mulla Sadra:

> This Reality [i.e. God] is not restricted by any definition, limitation, imperfection, contingent potentiality, or quiddity; nor is It mixed with any generality, whether of genus, species, or differentia, nor with any accident, whether specific or general. For Being is prior to all these descriptions that apply to quiddities, and That which has no quiddity other than Being is not bound by any generality or specificity ... For if His Being had some limit or particularity in any respect, It would have to be limited and particularized by something other than Being; there would have to be something with power over Him limiting, specifying, and circumscribing Him. But that is impossible.[44]

---

[44] Translation from Sadr al-Din Shirazi (1981, pp. 96, 100), quoted in Legenhausen (1986, p. 319).

God must truly stand alone – no nesting, no differentiation, and no category-mates allowed.

The way of difference may sound extreme. For it seems to entail – where *thing* is a wholly general category for any being whatsoever – that God is no thing, which would seem to entail that God is nothing, which would seem to entail that there is no God. This doesn't sound like a promising hypothesis for those who aspire to piety. It seems, in fact, to conflict with the existence component of monotheism. But proponents of the way of difference mean what they say. Thus David Bentley Hart:

> [It] is not, however, merely a distinction in numbering, between monotheism and polytheism, as though the issue were merely that of determining how many "divine entities" one happens to think there are. It is a distinction, instead, between two entirely different kinds of reality, belonging to two entirely disparate conceptual orders … To speak of "God" properly, then – to use the word in a sense consonant with the teachings of orthodox Judaism, Christianity, Islam, Sikhism, Hinduism, Bahá'í, a great deal of antique paganism, and so forth – is to speak of the one infinite source of all that is … God so understood is not something posed over against the universe, in addition to it, nor is he the universe itself. He is not a "being," at least not in the way that a tree, a shoemaker, or a god is a being; he is not one more object in the inventory of things that are, or any sort of discrete object at all.[45]

And Herbert McCabe:

> God must be incomprehensible to us precisely because he is creator of all that is and … [is] outside the order of all beings. God therefore cannot be classified as any kind of being. God cannot be compared to or contrasted with other things in respect of what they are like as dogs can be compared and contrasted with cats and both of them with stones or stars. God is not an inhabitant of the universe … When you have finished classifying and counting all the things in the universe you cannot add: "And also there is God." When you have finished classifying and counting everything in the universe you have finished, period. There is no God in the world.[46]

And Denys Turner:

> It might be objected that the oneness of God must be at least minimally mathematical … It might seem that there being one and only one God is, after all, just like my one pie for lunch, at least as far as it excludes there being two of them. The comparison is facile, though revealingly so. For that is exactly how not to think of the oneness of God … It is true that God's being "one" rules out there being two or more Gods. But this is not

---

[45] Hart (2013, pp. 28–30).   [46] McCabe (2005, p. 37)

for the reason that God's oneness excludes plurality in the same way as does the oneness of the just one pie excludes there being two of them. What is wrong with saying that there are two, or twenty-two, gods is not that you have added up the number of gods incorrectly. A plurality of gods is ruled out by God's oneness because God's oneness entails that counting is ruled out in every way.[47]

God is indeed no teacup in the cupboard of reality. And God isn't anything else within reality's domain either. And so God shares no categories at all with anything else.

Difference and Divine Attributes

Perhaps so. Perhaps the way of difference is the way of true and reverent theology; perhaps it alone gives due respect to the uniqueness of God.

But what about all the *other* things monotheists seem to believe and say about God? God is said to enjoy various features – divine attributes, as they say. What about the claim, for example, that God is perfectly just? This is more than a rhetorical question, and we need not stray far to find a potent argument. Consider this dilemma: either God is just or not. If God is indeed just, then God falls under a category with other things (other just things) – contra the way of difference. And if God is not just, then biblical or Quranic verses testifying to God's justice would be in error.

The dilemma at hand is, of course, of theoretical interest. It gives shape to a more general puzzle of whether created beings like us can say or believe anything at all – anything that is both true and informative, that is – about the Almighty.[48] What is less obvious, perhaps, is that the dilemma is of devotional interest too. For the attributes of God – think here of God's justice, for example – rightly figure into our own motivations for praying, adoring, listening to, and obeying God.

To be clear: I do not raise this dilemma to argue that the way of difference is incorrect. Rather, I raise it to foreground a problem that will occupy the rest of this Section. We can perhaps best approach that problem by first seeing how proponents of the way of difference respond to the dilemma. It is not as though they are unaware of it, after all. Though those proponents display some variety, a dominant mode of reply goes along these lines:

> According to Maimonides, God is absolutely transcendent and unknowable. There is not the faintest resemblance between him and his creatures. Maimonides explains that the anthropomorphic language of scripture is necessary for it is only by the use of such language that the masses of

---
[47] Turner (2013, pp. 11–12).   [48] Jacobs (2015).

people would be able to believe that God exists. When we say that God is just, this does not mean that God has the same attribute which we ascribe to just persons, but that God is not unjust and that he is the cause of all justice.[49]

You might have thought that sentences like "God is just" and "Solomon is just" both work in roughly the same way: they attribute a certain property – justice – to their subjects. It's a natural thought – but a mistake, say thinkers like Maimonides. For though both statements are indeed true, they do not both predicate one and the same property of their respective subjects. How does this work exactly? Here there is variety in formal machinery and detail. Perhaps, for example, the word "God" (or its cognates and synonyms in other languages) in the subject position somehow shifts the content of the rest of the words in a true target sentence, so "is just" denotes something different in the sentence "God is just" than it does in the sentence "Solomon is just." The property that "Solomon is just" attributes to Solomon would not, then, be the property attributed to God by "God is just." The precise semantic machinery, again, is not our concern, and non-semantic machinery may do just as well.[50] What matters is that it enables the affirmation of the target sentences about God – sentences like "God is just" – without thinking that God thereby shares any category at all with anything else.

What I now want to ask is what the way of difference teaches us about arguments that concern our nature and God's.

Difference and Divine Thinking

We introduced the assumption of divine thinking by considering various things monotheists canonically *say* about God. For example: that God believes all truths or that God is angry at wickedness. These sayings appear to require divine mentality; to believe or to be angry is to think. And so there appears to be a straightforward inference from the canonical sayings to the assumption of divine thinking.

God believes that the sum of two and two is four and therefore thinks. The way of difference gives us no reason to question such inferences to divine mentality. But it recommends that we interpret the premises and conclusions in a peculiar way. To see why, consider a parallel claim about some human person: Solomon believes that the sum of two and two is four and therefore thinks. It might seem like affirming both of these inferences commits us to the further conclusion that Solomon and God therefore have something in common (the shared property of *thinking*, or membership within a shared

---
[49] Legenhausen (1986, p. 313).   [50] Brower (2008).

ontological category like *thinking thing*, for example). But it doesn't, on the way of difference. Though we may affirm with a straight face that God believes (or is angry, or is wise, etc.) and therefore thinks, none of these affirmations imply that we have anything in common with the Almighty. God's thoughts are not our thoughts.

Vertical Arguments Blocked

The assumption of divine thinking has thus far survived scrutiny, then. But as understood by the way of difference, it cannot play the role I've envisioned for it in prior Sections. To see why, consider:

> [It is] ... no surprise to anyone who thinks that human persons are made in God's image [that] ... there is something about the way God is that is like the way we are. In our view, some of these similarities are to be expressed as various facts about God and human persons, facts that capture what it means for both of us to be persons – immaterial substances with a rational nature.[51]

An intriguing thought. It appeals to a doctrine that is widely accepted by monotheists – that we are made in the image of God. And it derives from this doctrine a claim about our nature: that we, like God, are immaterial thinking things. We might pause to consider how to best understand the image of God, for there is significant diversity here within and across the great Abrahamic traditions. But for our purposes, a more abstract treatment will suffice. Notice that this argument is but one within an extended family of arguments that would take us from premises about the divine nature to conclusions about the nature of human persons. We can sketch their structure – using the second person for ease of presentation – along these lines:

God _____. If God _____, then you _____. Therefore, you _____.

Arguments in this family identify a divine attribute in their first premise. And in the second premise – perhaps because we are made in the image of God, perhaps for other reasons – that attribute is then transferred or projected onto a human person.

To make things more concrete, consider these ways of filling in the blanks: (a) is an immaterial thinking thing, (b) is a magical thinker – that is, possessed of mentality not tethered to the workings of any wholly material thing (c) is able, despite being wholly immaterial, to causally interact with the material world, (d) is able to think without a body, (e) is essentially immaterial.

---

[51] Moreland & Rae (2000, p. 157).

You can probably think of more ways of filling in the blanks – one for every key concept deployed in this Element so far, and more besides. Each of these ways of filling in the blanks generates a new *vertical* argument – an argument that would move from God down to us. Each brings us to some answer to the category, modal, or mentality questions by first considering answers to parallel questions about God

The way of difference is an in-principle blocker to all vertical arguments. It poses a dilemma for their second premise. Consider two specifications of the premise that *if God is a magical thinker, then you are a magical thinker*, for example:

1. If God is a magical thinker, then you are (in the same sense) a magical thinker.
2. If God is a magical thinker, then you are (in some different sense) a magical thinker.

The proponent of the way of difference will reject the first specification of the premise. What is true of God is never also true of something else. There are no shared properties or categories.

And there will be no reason at all to accept the second specification of the premise. For the premise on this specification would appear to involve equivocation: moving from God being one way to you being some *other* way. That is not a convincing move.

The problem here extends beyond arguments that explicitly take this vertical form; any descent at all from God's level to ours will face the dilemma. Take the claim that, since God thinks without a body, it is therefore possible for something to think without a body. We used this claim earlier to dispatch arguments derived from the naturalistic slogan that only material beings can think. But the claim faces the dilemma just as sharply as do explicitly vertical arguments. For the claim may be specified further:

1. Since God thinks without a body, it is therefore possible (in the same sense) for something to think without a body.
2. Since God thinks without a body, it is therefore possible (in the some other sense) for something to think without a body.

As before, the first specification falls flat on the way of difference: no shared categories. And as before, the second premise would appear to involve unacceptable equivocation: moving from some possibility involving God to some distinct possibility involving something else. The only way to preserve these lines is to specify that the "something" in each is none other than God Almighty. Well the resulting specification would then be true: who could disagree that, since God thinks without a body, it is therefore possible for God to think without a body? But one can't use a premise like *that* to get an interesting vertical argument going.

We have found, then, a rather interesting spanner in the works. Anyone who would reason from God to us faces an objection from the way of difference. Attention to the *mono* part of *monotheism* uncovers surprising barriers to cogent argument from God's nature to our own. For one leading exposition of that *mono* bit – one prominent explanation of the uniqueness of God – imposes a formidable blockade on vertical arguments and anything like them.

Here is something that immediately follows: no vertical argument succeeds. That much is obvious. And here is something that follows from *that*: no vertical argument with dualist conclusions succeeds. So in addition to the objections I've already identified to arguments that would move from God to us (the objections developed in Sections 2 and 3, that is), we've now found an in-principle blockade to any such arguments, even those no one has thought of before.

If the way of difference is true, that is.

Analogy

There is a wrinkle in all this. Perhaps, though our thoughts are not God's thoughts, our thoughts are *like* God's thoughts. And in general, perhaps, though no true statements about God and us involve strict sharing of one and the same property or ontological category, they involve sharing *similar* properties or categories.

This is the doctrine of analogical predication – ever the friend of proponents of the way of difference.[52] I don't believe it helps. I don't believe it will unblock the blocker we've discovered, that is. Consider, for example, how the analogical theorist would understand the premise that *if God is a magical thinker, then you are a magical thinker*, as deployed in a vertical argument. They would, I think, maintain that it could be true if specified as follows: "If God is a magical thinker, then you are (in some different but similar sense to God) a magical thinker." Once we've understood the premise in this way, the conclusion must be modified too, or it will no longer follow. The conclusion must be buttressed with the very same analogical qualification, that is: "Therefore you are (in some different but similar sense to God) a magical thinker."

---

[52] Alston (1993) includes helpful contemporary discussion of and references to historical sources. See also White (2010).

This conclusion does not, I submit, have much bite as things stand. For until some specific respect of similarity is identified and justified – some way in which God's magic is like our magic, as it were – it's hard to argue that the conclusion rules out anything of interest. It is hard, that is, to see that the conclusion would rule out the view that our mental properties are identical to our physical properties, that our mental properties are fully tethered to our physical properties, and so on.

The doctrine of analogical predication, then, does not – absent further and specific explication – rescue vertical arguments. It does not unblock the blocker.

4.4 Coda

We've encountered a tempting thought: that one can argue from God's nature to ours, and that the results will be broadly dualist in form. We've seen that there is some truth to that tempting thought. Some naturalist slogans simply will not do. But a number of promising *arguments* that would take us from views about the divine nature to dualist theories about our own are unsound. That was the central result of Sections 2 and 3. This Section has identified yet another barrier to those arguments and any others like them. If the way of difference is correct, then we share no categories at all with God and so cannot reason vertically.

Is the way of difference cogent, and correct, and as pious as it seems? Must God really be that dramatically different from all else? I will leave these questions open. If you're inclined to accept the way of difference, though, you have a new in-principle reason to reject the arguments for dualism canvased previously. And conversely, if you lean toward accepting arguments for dualism from our similarity to God, you have a new in-principle reason to find some alternative explication of the uniqueness of God. Perhaps the way of counting – or some other way altogether; we'll consider one more in the Section to follow – will do.

The failure of arguments for dualism incepts the intriguing thought that materialism might survive or even thrive under monotheism. Could this be correct? What are the costs and benefits of the peculiar and heterodox brand of materialism now in view? Those are the questions of the next and final section.

5 Heterodoxy

5.1 The Way of Value

We have already observed two explications of the uniqueness of God. We'll now consider a third; it deploys *value* in saying how God is unique. The approach, as we'll see, faces important challenges. It also suggests a way forward in thinking about our place in this world. For just as monotheism demands that God be special or elevated within the grand order of *all* things, reflection on our own nature shows that we enjoy similar elevation in the order of *natural* things.

Value is the most general positive status. Anything that is good in any sense at all falls under this capacious umbrella. Value at this most abstract level includes, we might say, the good, the true, and the beautiful. Value comes in degrees; some things are more valuable than others. A helpful connection may be this: Anselmian perfection or supreme value is the upper limit case of value. To be perfect in St. Anselm's sense is to be good to the highest (conceivable) degree that one exists. Many kinds of things can be valuable: displays of courage, sublime waterfalls, true beliefs, properly functioning dehumidifiers, delicious durians, elegant theories – and people.

With these preliminary remarks in place, we can state the way of value thus: God is unique because God is the most valuable item in the cupboard of reality. Indeed, God enjoys *infinite* value, in contrast to the merely *finite* value exemplified by every other dish and cup in that pantry. God is not merely the most valuable thing among other valuable things (a difference of degree); God is the one and only infinitely valuable thing (a difference of kind). A chart will illustrate (Figure 5).

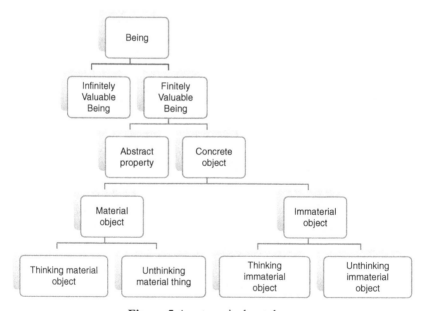

Figure 5 A categorical ontology

Two reasons recommend the way of value. First, it pays respect to the distinction between creator and creation. For the gap between infinitely valuable beings and finitely valuable beings is vast and deep. To see how wide the chasm extends, consider what it would take to *cross* it. We could add to the finite value of a painting a little bit every day, for example, by expanding its canvas or adding a tasteful detail here or there. We could do this for a million years. But even when additions and improvements build on each other, we'd still not bridge the gap. The finitely valuable painting would remain only finite in value: forever fundamentally different from an infinitely precious God. Monotheists convinced that God must be different in kind from all else will find this reassuring and correct.

Second, the way of value achieves this pious feat without much sacrifice in intelligibility. We may not know everything about infinity. But we do understand the ideas of *value*, of *degrees* of value, of *limits* to something's value, and thus by extension perhaps even of something having value *without any limit at all*. There is something deeply attractive about all this. God isn't just unique in some bare and factual sense; God is great and precious in some more evaluative sense as well.

5.2 Are We Infinitely Valuable Too?

The way of value is promising. Indeed, though I'll now challenge it, I'll argue that the challenge itself prompts some intriguing and useful questions about some of the results of our study thus far. These will set the stage for some programmatic remarks about a materialist metaphysics of human nature.[53]

My challenge, in brief, is that there is good reason to think that people are infinitely valuable too. So even if God is infinitely valuable, this is not a *unique* feature. I'll develop this idea in three steps. First: we human people are extremely and equally valuable. Second: this equal and extreme value calls out for explanation. Third: the best explanation is that we are infinitely valuable.

People: Extremely and Equally Valuable

Let's begin by thinking about the value of people. How much value does a human person have? At least some. You are valuable. You matter. It is good that you exist. Your value surpasses the value of many other things, including pugs, sunsets, twitterpation, valid arguments, delicious dinners, The Keeper of the Plains, and more. It is good that those items exist; the world is better for their being. Yet, there are important senses in which your value surpasses the value of beasts, landscapes, pleasant feelings, proofs, meals, or majestic steel sculptures. Your value is more extreme. You are no exception or outlier. I also enjoy this remarkable status. We *all* do. Value is our common human birthright.

---

[53] This section draws from considerably more rigorous (and purely secular) work in Rasmussen & Bailey (forthcoming).

We can be more specific. You may well be more effective than someone else when it comes to producing lucrative dance beats, for example, and thus more valuable in that *instrumental* sense. Or you might have powers of persuasion that make you a potent ally in campus politics. But when it comes to *final* value, you don't have more of that than anyone else. You are properly valued for your own sake exactly as much as anyone else. Here we are equals.

Explaining Equal and Extreme Value

Suppose that our value is indeed extreme and equal. This idea is puzzling. A parable:

> You are in a museum; paintings adorn the walls. Some appear lovely indeed. Others are plain. A curator approaches.
>
> "Did you know that every one of these paintings is a treasure, an artifact of deep value?"
>
> –"No."
>
> "It's true. And did you know that every one of these paintings enjoys exactly the same value as any other?"
>
> –"You must mean that they each have the same price. You'd charge the same amount to part ways with any of them."
>
> "Not quite. Art traders – their aim is lucre alone – talk about price and the conditions for voluntary exchange. But I'm talking about value. Each of these paintings has precisely the same value as any other – no more, no less!"
>
> –"Are you saying that, though these paintings differ in style and color and medium and era, each has the same power to generate good in the world, perhaps by arousing various reactions in viewers?"
>
> "That's not what I'm saying at all. Some of these paintings will produce all sorts of good in the hearts and minds of those who behold them. But others will leave their audiences empty. So I'm not talking about the equally valuable *effects* of these paintings. I'm saying that each of these paintings is equally valuable as an *end in itself*, regardless of its effects!"

The curator's claims are odd. The paintings differ wildly in their ability to generate positive affect (a kind of instrumental value). They differ wildly in many other respects, too. So how could it be that they are each finally valuable to the same degree? Some explanation is in order.

In the same way, some explanation is in order if all human beings are *extremely* and *equally* valuable. Like the paintings, we differ in color and size and shape. We differ in all manner of non-moral properties. We differ in all manner of moral properties too: some of us are well-behaved and disposed toward kindness or courage, others significantly less so. Like the paintings, we also differ wildly in our capacity to *produce* other kinds of goods – money, food, pleasure, awe, and so on. We differ in instrumental value in that sense. And yet, somehow we are indeed each *extremely* and *equally* valuable. How? Why?

Infinitely Valuable People

I think that the best answer is that we are all *infinitely* valuable. To see why, consider the contrasting hypothesis that the kind and degree of value we share is finite. To say this is to posit a wild and implausible coincidence. A final addition to the museum parable illustrates:

> As you prepare to take your leave from this strange place, the curator adds:
> "You seem to be skeptical about the deep and equal value of my paintings. So let me be more precise about how things stand. As it turns out, there's a large-ish unit of value – the axin (for reference, the median delicious meal clocks in at about 0.0004 axins). Every painting has precisely 61.2 axins of value. You can verify this claim by consulting an axinometer. I happen to have one right here if you'd like to use it!"

Would this additional detail make more explicable the thesis that each painting is extremely and equally valuable? It would not. It is all the more puzzling how these divergent paintings could have that same degree of final value. Indeed, for any finite amount of value, it would be strange indeed if each painting had precisely that degree of value. So also with people. It would be strange indeed if people all had great value to precisely the same finite degree. How could that be? What could explain or account for this apparent coincidence? Given our variation along other dimensions, the idea that we are all somehow exactly the same along this dimension is surprising and difficult to believe. Possible, yes – just like it is *possible* that all the paintings in our parable have the same degree of value. But surprising and unlikely.

The hypothesis that we are all infinitely valuable, by contrast, neatly explains our equal and extreme value. Infinity is a big number, so to speak, so no wonder we are *extremely* valuable; and value without limit is one unified *kind* of value, so to speak, so no wonder we are *equally* valuable. The hypothesis that we are infinitely valuable correctly predicts the data of extreme and equal value.

The argument I've sketched for the infinite value of people is by no means airtight, of course. Perhaps we aren't equally or extremely valuable in truth, for example, despite the usefulness of that fiction for modern liberal democracies. I'm not going to defend the assumption of equal and extreme value against that skeptical worry. But I will point out that the equal and extreme value of human beings can do much to explain a wide range of ethical phenomena. That we are *extremely* valuable nicely accounts for the deep wrongness of murder, for example. That we are *equally* valuable nicely accounts for the wrongness of inequitable treatment.

If all this is correct, then we stand alongside God on the infinite side of the value divide. Our value is just as without limit as God's is. Where one might have expected difference, we find instead similarity. Two things follow. First, we and God share an important category – that of infinitely valuable beings. So if God is special and set apart by virtue of exemplifying infinite value, we are too. This much sounds like good news. But note that, second, God would not be the only infinitely valuable being in town. God is special when contrasted with the rest of finite reality, to be sure. But God is not in this respect special when compared to us. What this shows, I think, is that the way of value faces a significant challenge. Proponents of the way of value must reject some premise of the argument that got us here – that we are equally valuable, for example, or that we are extremely valuable. I do not say that this route is utterly closed. But it does count against the way of value, I think. Despite its initial promise in setting up a vast divide between creator and creation, the way of value faces real difficulties.

There is a complication I must now briefly raise. Georg Cantor proved long ago that there are infinitely many infinities. Though there are infinitely many natural numbers and infinitely many real numbers, for example, there are more of the latter than the former. The way of value could be augmented in this way, then: perhaps, though human beings and God are alike in being infinitely valuable, the infinity that measures God's value is of a strictly higher cardinality.[54] The view is not without attractions, and it certainly improves on the way of value. Whether it might be the final and sober truth, however, is a matter we'll not settle here.

5.3 You Are Special

The way of value in its first form does not appear to succeed. But in bringing our focus to the value of God – and the value of people like you and me – it raises issues that I'd like to now address directly. In short, reflection on the way of value showed that there was reason to think that just as God is elevated among all things, we are elevated in some way too. When it comes to the natural world, we are special. Call me a speciesist if you like, but I simply don't think it can be maintained that everything else around you – this tree here, that desk there,

---

[54] On the theological consequences Cantor himself drew from his mathematical work, see Dauben (1977).

a book over there – is as special as you. Can this kernel of a thought grow into deeper insight about our own nature? I believe so.

You are a remarkable being. Here are just two ways in which this is true (I'm sure you can think of others). First, you are conscious. You can think and feel. There is something it is like to be you. Not everything is like that – take a look around you, for example and I suspect you'll see all sorts of things that can't think and feel. Your power to think and feel sets you apart in a striking way. Second, you are also extraordinarily valuable (something we've already discussed). You matter. It is good that you exist. There are both degreed and categorial elements to your value. Degreed: your value is extreme. You are very valuable. Categorial: you are also properly valued for your own sake, as an end. You have, that is, final value. Your value is also non-fungible: replacing you with an indistinguishable simulacrum – even a molecule-for-molecule duplicate – would deprive the world of something precious.[55] In this respect, as well, you are rather different from many other things in your environment.

And it's not just you. People in general – from teenagers to cognitivists to politicians and authors – are special.

Answers to the category, modality, and mentality questions would do well to respect the specialness of people. Plausible answers to the question of what we are will, at minimum, be compatible with the view that we are special indeed and set apart – somehow or other – from the rest of nature. And ideally, they'd go some way in saying *how* we're special too. They will, somehow or other, supply ontological backing to our special status. Here's what I mean. It is one thing to simply recite the dimensions along which we are special – I've mentioned two, consciousness and value. It is another to give a metaphysical account of how we enjoy these features and to say what, if anything, underlies or makes it the case that we have them. One classic move here, of course, is to posit an immaterial soul: that we have or are souls is said to account for our consciousness, our value, and thus to set us apart from nature. Materialists cannot resort to *this* kind of story. But there are other options, especially for the materialist willing to take on heterodox commitments.

We'll return to that thought. But before we do, I want to start consolidating and making more explicit some results from the arguments so far.

5.4 Materialism without Naturalism

Four broad views have played starring roles in this study: monotheism, materialism, dualism, and naturalism. Monotheism, recall, consists in the existence, supremacy, and uniqueness of God. Materialism says that we are wholly

---

[55] Crosby (2001), Zagzebski (2001).

material beings. Dualism says that we are at least partly immaterial. And naturalism says that the cosmos – the natural world – exhausts reality in its entirety and that everything is at root physical. Materialism and dualism answer the question of what we are by addressing the category question. They say we fall under the categories of *thinking material thing* and *thinking immaterial thing*, respectively. Monotheism and naturalism don't directly address the question of what we are. They operate instead at a more abstract level, each being something closer to a *worldview* or *grand ontological narrative*.

And yet monotheism and naturalism certainly bear on the question of what we are.

It would seem to many that monotheism, by virtue of its rejection of naturalism, would have some affinity to dualism. And naturalism would seem to favor materialism. While there is some truth to these hypotheses, we've seen that some arguments purporting to travel the route from monotheism to dualism do not succeed. Their failure shows that materialism is a surprisingly viable position for monotheists.

There is a more subtle result to highlight here as well. In saving materialism from various arguments for dualism, I have in fact deployed heterodox views – for naturalists, that is. The materialism I've saved is thus an oddball specimen – materialism without naturalism. Let me be more specific.

In answer to the category question, I have rejected the usual rigidity in favor of plasticity: our nature is flexible in that, though we're wholly material we could have been otherwise. And in answer to the mentality question, I have not insisted on the usual naturalistic slogans – that the mental depends on the physical, that the mental supervenes on the physical, that the mental is identical to the physical, and so on. I have eschewed commitment to the naturalist's usual tethering relations, that is. Instead, I have claimed that the materialist should be open, at least, to a magical view according to which our thoughts are not tethered to the physical properties of our bodies.

These plastic and magical augments to materialism are not just heterodox. They are anathema to the letter and spirit of naturalism. Plasticity is viable only given the supposition that there is (or could be, at least) something more than the cosmos and the purely natural order of things. To say that we could have been immaterial is to grant that there could have been immaterial things. And magical thinking is viable only if we reject – or at least are open to rejecting – the view that the physical world enjoys a priority in the order of things. If there could be mental properties that float free of the physical – thoughts not modally or explanatorily tethered to the material world – then not all facts are rooted within nature and the natural realm. Some facts – facts about what we're thinking, for example – would dangle somewhere beyond those borders.

Plasticity and magical thinking may come naturally enough to the monotheist, of course. With a supreme God on the loose, radical transformation that's otherwise downright unthinkable may seem possible indeed. And the existence of a mighty spirit suggests the possibility – and indeed, actuality – of magical thinking.

You may well wonder why the monotheist would want to adopt heterodox materialism in the first place. Sure, it shows surprising resistance to dualist arguments; but why not stick with dualism?

One answer is implicit in the arguments so far. Magical thinking has an advantage when it comes to Leibniz's thought experiment, for example. Magical materialists can give a precise diagnosis of where arguments in that neighborhood go wrong. They presuppose that there must be some *how* to things. But there isn't. The magical materialist thus has a way to resist a powerful argument for dualism. And indeed, adding heterodox magic to materialism generated a novel argument *for* materialism.

The point can be extended. The hard problem of consciousness – saying how the activity of material objects gives rise to our conscious experiences – is notoriously hard.[56] The magical materialist can give a simple and compelling account of why this is so. It is hard to give an elegant explanation, or any explanation really, of consciousness in physical terms because consciousness is not like the rest of the natural world. Consciousness is independent and magical. The magical materialist need not, let me emphasize, dogmatically *insist* on magic. There may be some pleasing, elegant, and unified structure to the connection between the physical and the mental, all captured by some simple equations. Perhaps so. Every once in a while, after all, a Newton stands tall and demonstrates that apparently complicated and disparate phenomena are in fact united under elegant and simple laws. Were a convincing theory of tethered thought to emerge, all would then be light. And the magical element of the heterodox materialism here in view would then be refuted or subject to serious qualification. But materialism would remain intact.

It may be objected that magical materialism is plainly absurd, outrageous, or unacceptable. I have no quarrel with this objection, for I suspect that any coherent position in the metaphysics of mind is absurd or outrageous or unacceptable.[57] Maybe the complaint is that magical materialism is an irresponsible refusal to inquire rather than a proper theory. "It's magic" sounds goofy and more like "angels did it" than "there are lawlike relations between the mental and the physical, which laws are captured by the following simple equation." Context matters here, though. The context of these arguments involves dualism and

---

[56] Chalmers (1995).   [57] Schwitzgebel (2014).

monotheism. If *those* views are to be taken seriously and count as live hypotheses, it is no less reasonable to give magical materialism a careful look.

I've focused in this Section on the magical element of magical materialism. There is a materialism element too. Since monotheists cannot help themselves to many of the usual naturalistic arguments for materialism, I'll say why they might be tempted to embrace materialism at all. It is on common sense grounds like these:

I have a height. I have mass, I take up space, and I've been seen. I've even been touched. These are obvious truths. They are obvious to non-philosophers, at least. And if they're true, I am a material object. For only a material object can have height, mass, take up space, and be seen. And only material objects can be touched. I am not alone in having height, mass, taking up space, and being seen. So human persons are material objects.

You might take this argument to begin with premises about sentences we ordinarily affirm or are disposed to affirm. That would not be a strong argument. Ordinary speech includes all sorts of sentences that aren't serious bits of metaphysics. A stronger argument would begin, not with a premise about what we say, but rather about, well, us. A premise like "we have each been seen and some of us occasionally bump into each other." Such a premise will, on reflection, seem true to many. And in a speculative metaphysical conversation where plasticity, magical thinking, dualism, or a divine spirit are on the table, we can't ask for much more than that.

A common sense case for materialism is compatible with monotheism. And if there's anything to this line of thought then monotheists have some reason to think that we are material beings, all without resorting to some broader naturalistic agenda.

5.5 Your Name in the Laws

I'll now introduce one more instance of a driving theme in this Element – that the rejection of naturalism and embrace of monotheism uncovers intriguing resources for developing and defending materialism. We'll begin with a story and the problem it illustrates.

The Lazarus Problem

Two thousand years ago, Lazarus of Bethany fell sick. To the sorrow of all who knew him, he then died. His body lay in a tomb and began to rot. But Lazarus was blessed with unusual friends; indeed, one of them was none other than Jesus of Nazareth. For four days his friends mourned dear Lazarus. For four days he was dead. But then Jesus approached the tomb and with a loud voice cried out: *Lazarus, come forth!* And Lazarus came forth, brought into new life.

Or so they say.[58]

Notice: Jesus did not merely bring some flesh and bone to life. He did not merely decree that *someone* would come forth – a decree that would be fulfilled were anyone at all to emerge, clothed in that reanimated body. Jesus brought *Lazarus himself* back to life. And there is a difference. For people aren't fungible; we cannot be swapped without loss. This is one way in which we are special, recall. To love *Lazarus* and hope for *him* to return is to hope for the return of a particular man, not just to hope that someone or other might emerge from that tomb using the body within.

I wonder how Jesus ensured that it was Lazarus himself who returned and not some other person. To ask this is not to wonder how Jesus of Nazareth managed to perform a miracle. There is no answer to that cheeky question. I wonder instead what, precisely, the miracle *was*. If dualism is true, the answer seems clear: Lazarus is or has a spirit. So, to bring Lazarus himself back is to once again unite that very spirit to some flesh and bone. Same spirit, same person.

It is significantly less clear what must be done if Lazarus neither has nor is a spirit – if materialism is true. To see the problem here consider a practical formulation. Suppose you have the power to configure matter and energy as you like. Say the word, and it is so. How would you make a human person? The answer seems to be along these lines: you'd arrange some matter and energy into the shape and configuration of a properly functioning human body and then let things unfold from there. If you'd done your job right, the newly formed body would, one hopes, begin breathing and so on. Once you "pressed play," as it were, the laws of nature that govern the interaction of cells and organs and atoms and electrons would come into effect and life would find a way.

How, though, would you make a *particular* human person? How would you see to it, not just that a new human person came into being, but that a *specific* person came into being? What could you do to ensure this result? If materialism is true, the answer is unclear. Arrange matter and energy as you like, and it is not at all obvious how you could ensure that the resulting human person would be Lazarus himself and not someone else who looked very much like Lazarus. The problem extends beyond resurrection; the question of how to ensure that a particular person is brought back to life is just an instance of this more general question: how do you see to it that a particular person is brought into being?

Recall the hard problem of consciousness: specifying how, if at all, the activity of physical items can give rise to conscious experience. The *Lazarus problem*, as I'll call it, lies in specifying how the activity of material beings can

---

[58] For the full story, see the eleventh chapter of St. John's Gospel.

give rise to a *particular* conscious *subject* of those experiences rather than some other subject. Where the former concerns the capacity of matter to support or somehow cause *experience*, the latter concerns the capacity of matter to support or somehow cause a particular *experiencer*.

Some think this is a problem for materialism. So Kenneth Einar Himma:

> The problem for the [materialist] is to explain how it is that the particular body that was born at a particular set of points in space-time (i.e. the first one born to my mother) creates *me* as a particular subject – and not someone else. In other words, the [materialist] must explain how, so to speak, the set of mereological simples arranged in the form of my body – or, more specifically, my brain – brings *me* into existence *qua* conscious subject, rather than someone else.[59]

Another instance of the Lazarus problem will further illustrate its generality and force. Martine Nida-Rümelin argues for dualism using this thought experiment: "Andrea's brain is divided into two halves, [and] each half is transplanted into a human body with the result of there being two people who are both psychologically continuous with the original person."[60] Here are three hypotheses about what happens: (a) Andrea is the woman associated with the body into which the left half was transplanted; (b) Andrea is the woman associated with the body into which the right half was transplanted, or (c) Andrea is associated with neither the left nor right body; Andrea does not survive the division and transplant operation.

There is a difference between (a) and (b). This much is obvious to Andrea when considering what her future might be like; to make that point vivid, just imagine you are Andrea and that you know the body on the left – but not the one on the right – will be imprisoned; you'd care a great deal in that case whether (a) or (b) is true. The dualist can clearly say where that difference lies: in scenario (a), Andrea's spirit has moved into or is embodied by the body on the left, and in (b), into the body on the right. Materialists, who deny that Andrea is or has a spirit, cannot tell this story. And it is unclear, says Nida-Rümelin, that they have any story to tell at all. For it doesn't seem as though any facts about the arrangement of matter or energy could account for the difference between (a) and (b); the bodies on the left and right are physically indistinguishable, let us say – each a close (though not perfect – they are in different places and have different histories, after all) simulacrum of the other.

Nida-Rümelin's argument exemplifies the Lazarus problem; it points to a scenario in which there are singular facts about *which particular person exists*

---

[59] Himma (2011, p. 434).

[60] Nida-Rümelin (2013, p. 703). See also Swinburne (2019, pp. 69–70).

or *where a specific person is* that are not settled by the physical facts. What Andrea wants to know is not merely whether someone or other is to be found in the bodies on the left and right – a general claim. She wants to know which one would be *her* – a singular claim.

A Singular Solution

The Lazarus problem is indeed a problem. But I'll now show that it can be resolved without embracing dualism. The way forward lies in reflecting on the powers of a supreme God and the singular and non-fungible regard God might display toward particular people. My proposal here will be speculative; I do not insist that it is the full and sober truth. But its coherence will show that the Lazarus problem need not leave materialists in stunned silence. If there is a supreme God, the Lazarus problem isn't insurmountable.

Begin with God. Not just any will do; we'll need the almighty God of monotheism. For the God I'm thinking of here doesn't just have some localized or limited power over parcels of matter or energy. The God I'll recruit is, rather, supreme in this sense: God is intimately involved with the very laws of nature. Those rules that govern the cosmos are nothing less than God's standing dispositions toward nature and how it is to unfold.[61] It is a law of nature that massive objects attract, for example, because, in an ongoing fashion and in a regular and systematic way, God is disposed to bring about the attraction of massive objects.

Laws of nature are widely thought to be general. You could write them out, as it were, without using proper names. They govern nature by broad decree. I think that is correct, as far as things go. The rules that govern mass and attraction encode God's fungible dispositions toward the attraction of massive objects. They are indifferent as to *which* objects in particular are massive or attractive.

I propose that, in addition to such general laws there are singular laws that pertain to particular people. "Whenever such-and-such physical properties are instantiated," such a singular law might say, "the thing that has those properties is Jo herself." Or "whenever some neurons are arranged thus-and-so, the organism of which they are a part is Bo himself."[62]

Laws connect one state to another. A law might bridge between a physical state of fundamental particles to a chemical state of the molecule they compose, for example; a law like that would help explain why anything in that physical

---

[61] On laws as divine intentions, see Ratzsch (1987).

[62] For proposals similar in spirit to the one I float here, see Brenner (forthcoming) and Yang & Davis (2017).

state is also in the chemical state.[63] My hypothesis is that some laws connect physical states to states that essentially involve particular individuals. Such singular laws would help explain why those particular individuals are implicated by the underlying physical state. And the laws themselves would be explained by God. So I do not propose that it is a *brute* or *unexplained* fact that certain physical configurations give rise to Bo. Rather, God has – perhaps out of love for Bo or an intention to bring Bo in particular into being – instituted a standing decree that should those physical conditions obtain, Bo exists. It is God and God's care for particular creatures that ultimately explains why they come to be: a fitting result given the supremacy of God.

An analogy may help illustrate the distinction between general and singular rules. A general criminal law against theft goes like this: "Anyone who steals shall be imprisoned." A singular criminal law against theft says instead: "If Petra steals, she shall be imprisoned." Criminal laws tend toward generality, of course – and rightly so. So also the laws of nature with which we are familiar.

But I'm proposing that, in addition to all the usually countenanced laws of nature, there are also rules that speak to people in particular, given certain physical conditions. How many singular laws are there? Enough to go around, I hypothesize. God's standing intentions for how the cosmos unfolds speak to each of us, individually. Indeed, all of us are the singular subjects of our very own laws. The rules that govern the cosmos call us out by name.

And so, unlike other natural rules – or most criminal laws – you couldn't write out the laws about us without, as it were, using proper names. If the laws of nature are God's hands, the instruments of supreme rule, we are graven into those mighty palms.

The idea of singular laws encodes something many have found plausible: that God has non-fungible regard for particular people. We are not all the same to God; and God doesn't just make decrees about or care for or love or punish people in general. God does those things with respect to particular people. God didn't just choose some ancient person or other, for example. God chose *Abraham*. I propose that God's singular and non-fungible regard for people extends all the way into the rules that govern the cosmos. God picked the laws of nature that would, in concert with the activity of the cosmos, bring into being precisely those people God ordained. Some argue that the cosmos is fine-tuned for life; my conjecture is that God has fine-tuned the laws *for the lives of specific people*.

That God should care so much for each of us in particular is an exhilarating thought. It has theoretical payoffs too. Singular laws link between the multifarious

---

[63] On laws and metaphysical explanation, see Schaffer (2018)

arrangements of matter and energy and the coming to be (or resurrection, or location) of particular people. *How* does Jesus bring about the resurrection of Lazarus himself, and not merely that of some simulacrum? By arranging matter and energy in some way such that, conjoined with a singular law, entails that the resulting person is Lazarus himself. The singular law encodes a standing intention God has toward Lazarus himself. Jesus' miraculous transformation of the matter and energy in the tomb "activates" this singular law, if you like.

We can generalize the point. Recall the Lazarus problem: saying why or how activity of material beings can give rise to a particular conscious subject of those experiences rather than some other subject. With singular laws in hand, the materialist can resolve the puzzle. The activity of some material beings gives rise to Bo rather than Jo because the laws say so; and the laws say so because they are divine decrees expressing God's non-fungible intention that Bo, in particular, should be. The singular resolution now in view applies to Himma's argument as follows: your particular body gives rise to *you* because God decreed that it should be so. Perhaps God could have decreed otherwise – in that case, a perfect simulacrum of your body would have given rise to someone else – again because God decreed that it should be so. Nida-Rümelin's argument may be answered along similar lines. If there is a difference between scenarios (a) and (b) it is this: should Andrea be the woman associated with the body on the left, this would be a consequence of a singular and divinely decreed law that linked Andrea herself to the physical properties instantiated by the body on the left.

There are, I've said, enough singular laws to go around – and they implicate all of us by name. This may appear to involve outrageous theoretical complexity.[64] But the point doesn't tell against the materialist. For the dualist must make a very similar move herself in answering the Lazarus problem and saying how a body gives rise to some particular spirit rather than another. Whatever machinery is invoked here – special divine decrees that connect particular bodies to particular spirits, for example – will bear a striking resemblance to the singular laws I have discussed.[65] The materialist incurs no unique cost in making use of singular laws.

The proposal I've floated here – singularity, in a word – is not strictly incompatible with naturalism. But it would be somewhat inexplicable were naturalism true. It wouldn't surprise the monotheist that a supreme God – endowed with full command over the laws of nature, who cares for individuals as such – should write people into the rules governing the cosmos. It would be

---

[64] Collins (2011, pp. 234–35).

[65] Dualists who explicitly endorse the possibility of singular causal laws include Foster (1991, p. 167) and Unger (2005, ch. 7).

much more surprising, were there no God, for the laws to call us out by name. So I do not claim that singular laws are totally unavailable to the naturalist. But they do comport better with monotheism.

5.6 Conclusion

Materialism, when augmented with plasticity, magic, and singularity, can flourish. For those heterodox supplements to materialism undermine key dualist arguments. They can also help the materialist say how we are special.

The observation that we are special is, I think, in some initial tension with materialist answers to the question of what we are. On such views, we stand in continuous solidarity with the rest of nature. We are, like stars and rocks, wholly material – made of the same stuff, obeying the same laws, and so on. There's something pleasing and orderly about all this. Minds attracted to systems and cogs and wheels within wheels, at least, will be drawn to a materialism that places us within nature's grand machine. But locating us in the material world can falsely suggest that we are all too ordinary. A speech will illustrate:

You may locate us entirely within the material world if you like, made of the same stuff as stars and rocks. Naturalists have been saying these things for years, but they come at a price. To affirm materialism is to abandon our uniqueness in the natural order and, ultimately, to strip our lives of meaning, significance, purpose, or value. For on these doctrines, we are no more special than rocks or stars, no more valuable than protozoa or prairie dogs. Believe all that if you can; I for one, cannot. I say that we're special, and that our special status lies in this fact: we have or are souls.

We could think of this speech as an argument against materialism. Put that way, I don't think it is all that convincing. But there is still something to it, and it deserves a reply. The materialist would still do well to specify how we are special. The theses of plasticity, magic, and singularity suggest such a reply:

We are indeed wholly material beings. But we're not like everything else. We are, as you say, special. For we are uniquely plastic, magical, and singular. Plastic: we could have been immaterial. Magical: our thinking is not tethered to our physical properties. Singular: the laws speak to each of us in particular and not merely by general decree. The view that we're not all that different from rocks or stars is a mistake. For we can do things that rocks can't – survive a transformation into pure immateriality, for example. We have special properties – conscious mental properties, thoughts, feelings – that aren't modally or explanatorily tied to the properties of our parts. And we figure into the laws as individuals, unlike anything else of which we know. Though we're made of the same stuff as rocks, plasticity, magic, and singularity mark important metaphysical differences that divide us from the rest of nature.

The reply has two important elements. First, there's a claim to *uniqueness*. If plasticity, magic, and singularity are features that set us apart from nature, then they can't be had by just any old thing. And second, there's the claim to *elevation*. If plasticity, magic, and singularity are to set us apart in a way that makes us *special*, they must not merely be unique. They must confer value or positive status. Though I find the uniqueness and elevation claims plausible, I will not argue here that they are true. My point is more abstract: here is a new way forward for materialists. Instead of proceeding from a commitment to naturalism, a materialist answer to the category question may be defended by rejecting orthodox naturalistic answers to the modality and mentality questions or by positing singular laws. Embracing heterodoxy on these fronts points toward new ways of showing how we are special and elevated, all without breathing a word about immaterial souls.

Here's how Lynne Rudder Baker puts things:

> That human persons are in some respects unique is indisputable; everything is unique in some respects. What is controversial is whether persons are onto-logically unique ... I submit that our being persons is the deepest fact about us: the properties peculiar to persons are sufficiently different from the properties of nonpersons to warrant the conclusion that persons – with their inner lives that spawn memoirs, confessions, autobiographies, etc. – are a unique kind of being. No other kind of being has values that lead to the great cultural achievements of science, technology, government, the arts, religion, morality, and the production of wealth. The variety and sophistica-tion of the products of human endeavor are good evidence for the ontological uniqueness of persons.[66]

I think Baker is right. People are special. And this specialness must somehow be marked in an ontology of human persons. Rejecting naturalistic orthodoxy – and opting instead for plasticity, magical thinking, or singularity – is an intri-guing way to do this. I'm not convinced that it can succeed. Each of these heterodox proposals has a speculative air to it; these are uncertain metaphysical waters. But I think I've shown that they have significant promise. Anyone interested in developing a materialist answer to the question of what we are would do well to further explore heterodox and non-naturalistic augmentations. Monotheists, having already rejected naturalism, will find that program unusually attractive.

It is time to conclude this Element. We began by wondering how the exist-ence, supremacy, and uniqueness of an almighty and immaterial God bear on our own nature. Are there lessons about what we are from reflecting on what

---

[66] Baker (2007, p.90).

God is? I have argued in the affirmative. Abrahamic monotheism, as it turns out, is a surprisingly hospitable framework within which to defend and develop a materialist metaphysics of human nature. But the resulting materialism is heterodox – it demands revisions and twists on the usual naturalistic views. It holds that our nature, in contrast to that of more ordinary material objects, is plastic; and it is open to the view that our thoughts are nothing less than magic. We can indeed learn about ourselves by learning about God. One thing we learn is that, though we are indeed wholly material beings, we're not nearly as ordinary as we might seem.

References

Alston, William P. (1993). Aquinas on theological predication. In Eleonore Stump, ed., *Reasoned Faith: Essays in Philosophical Theology in Honor of Norman Kretzmann*. Cornell University Press.

Al-Ghazali, A. H. M. (2005). *Al-Ghazali on Divine Essence: A Translation from the Iqtisad Fi Al-I-Tiqad with Notes and Commentary*, trans. Dennis Morgan Davis, Jr.University of Utah Press.

Aquinas, Thomas (1947). *Summa Theologiae*, 3 vols., trans. The Fathers of the English Dominican Province. Benziger Brothers.

Audi, Paul (2011). Primitive causal relations and the pairing problem. *Ratio* 24: 1–16.

Bailey, Andrew (2015). The priority principle. *Journal of the American Philosophical Association* 1 (1): 163–74.

Bailey, Andrew (2017). On the concept of a spirit. *Religious Studies* 53 (4): 449–57.

Bailey, Andrew (2020a). Magical thinking. *Faith and Philosophy* 37 (2): 181–201.

Bailey, Andrew (2020b). Material through and through. *Philosophical Studies* 177 (8): 2431–50.

Baker, Lynne Rudder (2007). *The Metaphysics of Everyday Life: An Essay in Practical Realism*. Cambridge University Press.

Block, Ned (1995). On a confusion about a function of consciousness. *Behavioral and Brain Sciences* 18: 227–47.

Bowers, Jason (2019). A teleological answer to the special composition question. *Dialectica* 73: 231–46.

Brenner, Andrew (forthcoming). How to be a mereological anti-realist. Oxford Studies in Philosophy of Religion.

Brower, Jeffrey (2008). Making sense of divine simplicity. *Faith and Philosophy* 25 (1): 3–30.

Burns, Elizabeth (2015). "Classical and revisionary theism on the divine as personal: A rapprochement?" *International Journal for Philosophy of Religion* 78: 151–165.

Carruthers, Peter (2004). *The Nature of the Mind*. Routledge.

Chalmers, David (1995). Facing up to the problem of consciousness. *Journal of Consciousness Studies* 2 (3): 200–19.

Cole, David & Robert Foelber (1984). Contingent materialism. *Pacific Philosophical Quarterly* 65: 74–85.

Collins, Robin (2011). A scientific case for the soul. In Mark C. Baker and Stewart Goetz, eds., *The Soul Hypothesis: Investigations Into the Existence of the Soul*. Continuum.

Crosby, John F. (2001). The twofold source of the dignity of persons. *Faith and Philosophy* 18: 292–306.

Cucu, Alin & J. Brian Pitts (2019). How dualists should (not) respond to the objection from energy conservation. *Mind and Matter* 17 (1): 95–121.

Dauben, Joseph W. (1977). Georg Cantor and Pope Leo XIII: Mathematics, theology, and the infinite. *Journal of the History of Ideas* 38 (1): 85–108.

Davies, Brian (2004). *An Introduction to the Philosophy of Religion*, 3rd ed. Oxford University Press.

Foster, John (1991). *The Immaterial Self*. Oxford University Press.

Hart, David Bentley (2013). *The Experience of God: Being, Consciousness, Bliss*. Yale University Press.

Hart, W. D. (1988). *The Engines of the Soul*. Cambridge University Press.

Hasker, William (2010). Persons and the unity of consciousness. In George Bealer and Robert Koons, eds., *The Waning of Materialism: New Essays*. Oxford University Press.

Herbener, Jens-André (2013). On the term "Monotheism." *Numen* 60: 616–48.

Himma, Kenneth (2011). Explaining why this body gives rise to me qua subject instead of someone else: An argument for classical substance dualism. *Religious Studies* 47 (4): 431–48.

Hoffman, Joshua & Gary S. Rosenkrantz (1997). *Substance: Its Nature and Existence*. Routledge.

Jacobs, Jonathan (2015). The ineffable, inconceivable, incomprehensible God: Fundamentality and apophatic theology. *Oxford Studies in Philosophy of Religion* 6: 158–76.

Kim, Jaegwon (2005). *Physicalism, or Something Near Enough*. Princeton University Press.

LaRock, Eric & Robin Collins (2016). Saving our souls from materialism. In Thomas M. Crisp, Steven Porter, and Gregg A. Ten Elshof, eds., *Neuroscience and the Soul*. Eerdmans.

Legenhausen, Gary (1986). Is God a person? *Religious Studies* 22: 307–23.

Leibniz, G. W (1951). *Leibniz Selections*, ed. Philip Weiner. Charles Scribner's Sons.

Lowe, E. J. (2000). *Introduction to the Philosophy of Mind*. Cambridge University Press.

Lowe, E. J. (2010). Substance dualism: A non-cartesian approach. In George Bealer and Robert Koons, eds., *The Waning of Materialism: New Essays*. Oxford University Press.

Maimonides, Moses (1974). *The Commentary of R. Hoter Ben Shelomo to the Thirteen Principles of Maimonides*, trans. David R. Blumenthal.Brill.

McCabe, Herbert (2005). *God Still Matters*. Continuum.

Merricks, Trenton (1994). A new objection to a priori arguments for dualism. *American Philosophical Quarterly* 31: 81–85.

More, Henry (1660). *An Explanation of the Grand Mystery of Godliness.* London. https://quod.lib.umich.edu/e/eebo/A51302.0001.001?rgn=main; view=fulltext

Moreland, J.P. (2013). A conceptualist argument for a spiritual substantial soul. *Religious Studies*, 49: 35–43.

Moreland, J. P. (2018). In defense of a Thomistic-like dualism. In Jonathan Loose, Angus Menuge, and J. P. Moreland, eds., *The Blackwell Companion to Substance Dualism.* Wiley-Blackwell.

Moreland, J. P. & Scott B. Rae (2000). *Body & Soul: Human Nature & the Crisis in Ethics.* 3rd paperback ed. InterVarsity Press.

Mullins, Ryan (2020). *God and Emotion.* Cambridge University Press.

Ney, Alyssa. (2008). Defining physicalism. *Philosophy Compass* 3: 1033–48.

Nida-Rümelin, Martine (2013). The argument for subject body dualism from transtemporal identity defended. *Philosophy and Phenomenological Research* 86 (3): 702–14.

Oppy, Graham (2014). *Describing Gods: An Investigation of Divine Attributes.* Cambridge University Press.

Owen, Matthew (forthcoming). Circumnavigating the causal pairing problem with hylomorphism and the integrated information theory of consciousness. *Synthese.*

Place, U. T. (1956). Is consciousness a brain process? *British Journal of Psychology* 47: 44–50.

Plantinga, Alvin (1974). *The Nature of Necessity.* Oxford University Press.

Plantinga, Alvin (2006). Against materialism. *Faith and Philosophy* 23 (1): 3–32.

Plantinga, Alvin (2007). Materialism and Christian belief. In Dean Zimmerman and Peter van Inwagen, eds., *Persons: Human and Divine.* Oxford University Press.

Rasmussen, Joshua (2018). Against nonreductive physicalism. In Jonathan Loose, Angus Menuge, and J. P. Moreland, eds., *The Blackwell Companion to Substance Dualism.* Wiley-Blackwell.

Rasmussen, Joshua & Andrew Bailey (forthcoming). "How valuable could a person be?" *Philosophy and Phenomenological Research.*

Ratzsch, Del (1987). Nomo(theo)logical necessity. *Faith and Philosophy* 4 (4): 383–402.

Rosen, Gideon (2012). Abstract objects. In *The Stanford Encyclopedia of Philosophy.* https://plato.stanford.edu/entries/abstract-objects/

Sadr al-Din Shirazi (1981). *The Wisdom of the Throne*, trans. James Winston Morris. Princeton University Press.

Schaffer, Jonathan (2018). Laws for metaphysical explanation. *Royal Institute of Philosophy Supplement* 82: 1–22.

Schwitzgebel, Eric (2014). The crazyist metaphysics of mind. *Australasian Journal of Philosophy* 92: 665–82.

Segal, Aaron (forthcoming). Dependence, transcendence, and creaturely freedom: On the incompatibility of three theistic doctrines. *Mind*.

Segal, Aaron & Tyron Goldschmidt (2017). The necessity of idealism. In Tyron Goldschmidt and Kenneth L. Pearce, eds., *Idealism: New Essays in Metaphysics*. Oxford University Press.

Smart, J. J. C. (1959). Sensations and brain processes. *The Philosophical Review* 68: 141–156.

Smith, Peter & O. R. Jones (1986). *The Philosophy of Mind*. Cambridge University Press.

Swinburne, Richard (1997). *The Evolution of the Soul*, revised ed. Oxford University Press.

Swinburne, Richard (2019). *Are We Bodies or Souls?* Oxford University Press.

Taliaferro, Charles (1994). *Consciousness and the Mind of God*. Cambridge University Press.

Taliaferro, Charles (1997). Possibilities in philosophy of mind. *Philosophy and Phenomenological Research* 57: 127–137.

Tuggy, Dale (2017). On counting gods. *TheoLogica* 1: 188–213.

Turner, Denys (2013). *Thomas Aquinas: A Portrait*. Yale University Press.

Unger, Peter (2005). *All the Power in the World*. Oxford University Press.

van Inwagen, Peter (1990). *Material Beings*. Cornell University Press.

van Inwagen, Peter (2002). What do we refer to when we say "I"? In Jonathan Loose, Angus Menuge, and J. P. Moreland, eds., *The Blackwell Guide to Metaphysics*. Wiley-Blackwell.

van Inwagen, Peter (2014). What is an ontological category? In *Existence: Essays in Ontology*. Oxford University Press.

van Inwagen, Peter (2015). *Metaphysics*, 4th ed. Westview Press.

White, R. M. (2010). *Talking about God: The Concept of Analogy and the Problem of Religious Language*. Ashgate.

Willard, Dallas (1999). *The Divine Conspiracy: Rediscovering Our Hidden Life in God*. HarperOne.

Yang, Eric T. & Stephen T. Davis (2017). Composition and the will of God: Reconsidering resurrection by assembly. In T. Ryan Byerly and Eric J. Silverman, eds., *Paradise Understood: New Philosophical Essays About Heaven*. Oxford University Press.

Zagzebski, Linda (2001). The uniqueness of persons. *Journal of Religious Ethics* 29: 401–423.

Acknowledgments

The central ideas of this Element fermented for years through conversation with many, including Brad Rettler, Alex Arnold, Mike Rea, Nathan Ballantyne, Allison Krile Thornton, Peter van Elswyk, Amy Seymour, Eric Yang, Alex Skiles – and above all, with my fellow traveller and sometimes co-author, Josh Rasmussen. Thank you all for the love you have shown to me in the language philosophers know best: one objection, then another. I'm also grateful to the editors of this series for the chance to write, to anonymous referees for helpful comments, and to my trusty research assistant, Joseph Han, for extensive feedback on the manuscript.

This is a work of speculative philosophical theology. Its conjectures are unaided – by scriptures, yes, but also by scholarly tradition, textual commentary, or analytic nuance and technique. I hope to, in future articles, develop some of these ideas with the help of my own home tradition and academic discipline. Speaking of articles: ancestors of a few arguments here have appeared in print; I thank *Faith and Philosophy*, *Religious Studies*, and *Philosophy and Phenomenological Research* for permission to deploy streamlined and updated excerpts here.

I offer final thanks to Jan May for her indefatigable love and support, which sustained me in writing even when other helps gave way. I dedicate this Element to the first graduating class of Yale-NUS College – the Class of 2017. It's been an adventure, friends.

Cambridge Elements ≡

Religion and Monotheism

Paul K. Moser

Loyola University Chicago

Paul K. Moser is Professor of Philosophy at Loyola University Chicago. He is the author of *Understanding Religious Experience*; *The God Relationship*; *The Elusive God* (winner of national book award from the Jesuit Honor Society); *The Evidence for God*; *The Severity of God*; *Knowledge and Evidence* (all Cambridge University Press); and *Philosophy after Objectivity* (Oxford University Press); co-author of *Theory of Knowledge* (Oxford University Press); editor of *Jesus and Philosophy* (Cambridge University Press) and *The Oxford Handbook of Epistemology* (Oxford University Press); co-editor of *The Wisdom of the Christian Faith* (Cambridge University Press). He is the co-editor with Chad Meister of the book series *Cambridge Studies in Religion, Philosophy, and Society*.

Chad Meister

Bethel University

Chad Meister is Professor of Philosophy and Theology and Department Chair at Bethel College. He is the author of *Introducing Philosophy of Religion* (Routledge, 2009), *Christian Thought: A Historical Introduction*, 2nd edition (Routledge, 2017), and *Evil: A Guide for the Perplexed*, 2nd edition (Bloomsbury, 2018). He has edited or co-edited the following: *The Oxford Handbook of Religious Diversity* (Oxford University Press, 2010), *Debating Christian Theism* (Oxford University Press, 2011), with Paul Moser, *The Cambridge Companion to the Problem of Evil* (Cambridge University Press, 2017), and with Charles Taliaferro, *The History of Evil* (Routledge 2018, in six volumes).

About the Series

This Cambridge Element series publishes original concise volumes on monotheism and its significance. Monotheism has occupied inquirers since the time of the Biblical patriarch, and it continues to attract interdisciplinary academic work today. Engaging, current, and concise, the Elements benefit teachers, researchers, and advanced students in religious studies, Biblical studies, theology, philosophy of religion, and related fields.

Cambridge Elements ⁼

Religion and Monotheism

Printed in the United States
by Baker & Taylor Publisher Services